Picturing India

JOHN McALEER

Picturing India

BRITISH LIBRARY

PEOPLE, PLACES AND THE WORLD
OF THE EAST INDIA COMPANY

Picturing India: People, Places and the World of the East India Company
John McAleer

First published 2017 by
The British Library
96 Euston Road
London NW1 2DB

ISBN 978 0 7123 5695 4

Designed by Maggi Smith, Sixism
Printed in China by C & C Offset Printing Co.

On the jacket: William Simpson, *The Palace at Amber*, c. 1861
(see Fig. 3.20)

Pages 2–3: Detail of Fig. 2.5

All images are from the collection of the British Library unless
stated otherwise in the captions. 'YCBA' is the Yale Center for
British Art, New Haven.

Contents

Acknowledgements

This book owes its existence to Rebecca Nuotio and Rob Davies at the British Library. Without their interest and enthusiasm for this project at the outset, and their unfailing encouragement along the way, a throwaway comment made during a conversation in one of the Library's cafes would have remained just that.

During the course of writing this book, I benefited from the help and assistance of a variety of libraries, librarians and archivists. I am grateful to Nick Graffy at the Hartley Library and to his colleagues in the Inter-library Loan Department at the University of Southampton. I would also like to thank Penny Brook, Margaret Makepeace and all of their colleagues in the India Office Records at the British Library for their generous assistance and guidance. I am particularly grateful to Mark Pomeroy and his colleagues at the Royal Academy, London, for permission to consult and quote from the papers of Ozias Humphry. Finally, as ever, I relied heavily on the staffs of the British Library, London, and the Hartley Library at the University of Southampton.

As always, I am grateful to those friends and colleagues who have helped me to think about the East India Company and the images it inspired over the years: Tim Barringer, Robert Blyth, Huw Bowen, Quintin Colville, James Davey, Douglas Fordham, Gillian Forrester, Douglas Hamilton, Sarah Longair, Philip McEvansoneya, John MacKenzie, Margaret Makepeace, Peter (P. J.) Marshall, John Oldfield, Katherine Prior, Geoff Quilley, Johanna Roethe and Zoë White. Many of them read drafts of chapters or listened to papers. I am grateful for their help and advice, although naturally any errors or omissions are mine. Thanks in particular to Johanna who read drafts of all the chapters with great insightfulness and unfailing cheerfulness.

This book is about the images. Although the shortcomings and inadequacies of the text are my sole responsibility, the book is the product of significant amounts of collective effort and dedication. I am grateful to Sally Nicholls for her help in sourcing the images. On behalf of everyone who admires the high-quality illustrations, I would like to acknowledge and thank everybody in the Imaging Services department at the British Library who ensured that the images are the real stars of the book. I am also very grateful to Jacqueline Harvey for her careful reading of the text and to the book's designer, Maggi Smith, for turning an idea into reality. Where I have quoted directly from a source, the endnotes provide specific references. Readers who are interested in pursuing some of the themes explored in these pages will find suggestions for further reading at the end of the book.

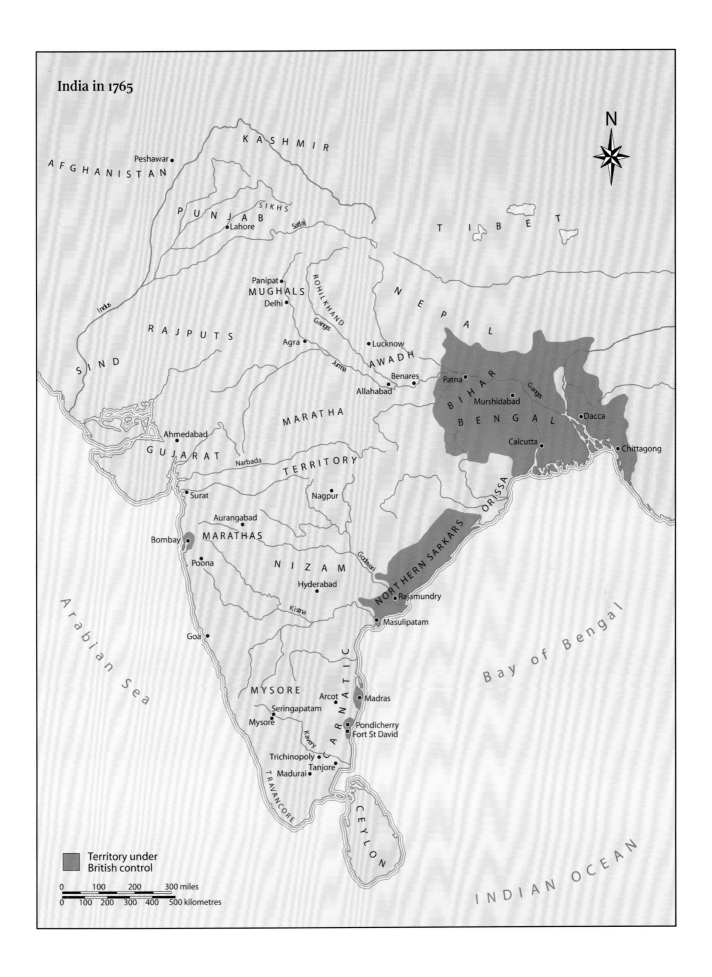

India in 1765

N

KASHMIR
AFGHANISTAN
Peshawar

PUNJAB
SIKHS
Lahore
Sutlej
Indus

TIBET

Panipat
MUGHALS
Delhi
ROHILKHAND
NEPAL

RAJPUTS
Ganges
Agra
Lucknow
AWADH
SIND
Jumna
Benares
Allahabad
Patna
BIHAR
Murshidabad
Ganges
Dacca

MARATHA
BENGAL
Ahmedabad
Calcutta
Chittagong
GUJARAT
Narbada
TERRITORY
ORISSA

Surat
Nagpur
Aurangabad

Bombay
MARATHAS
NORTHERN SARKARS
Poona
NIZAM
Godavari
Hyderabad
Rajamundry
Kistna
Masulipatam
Goa

Bay of Bengal

Arabian Sea

MYSORE
Arcot
Madras
Seringapatam
CARNATIC
Mysore
Pondicherry
Fort St David
Kaveri
Trichinopoly
Tanjore
Madurai
TRAVANCORE

CEYLON

Territory under
British control

0   100   200   300 miles
0   100 200 300 400   500 kilometres

INDIAN OCEAN

The East India Company and British Views of India

Eighteenth-century India was 'the theatre of scenes highly important' to Britain.[1] So wrote the artist and traveller William Hodges. He was in a good position to judge. Hodges was one of the first British professional landscape painters to visit India, spending six years there under the patronage of Warren Hastings, the most important British official in the subcontinent. As well as painting portraits and creating other works for Hastings, Hodges undertook extensive travels throughout India. And all of these experiences were documented in sketches and drawings, many of which were later worked up into finished oil paintings or published as prints (Fig. 1.1).

In matters of trade and war, the Indian subcontinent had assumed an increasingly important role in British political and economic life in the second half of the eighteenth century. This relationship between Britain and India was complex and had its roots in the activities of a London-based trading company. The 'Company of Merchants of London, trading to the East Indies' – usually abbreviated as the East India Company – controlled British trade with Asia from its foundation in 1600 until the nineteenth century, and was once described as 'the wealthiest and most powerful commercial corporation of ancient or modern times'. Any examination of Britain's relationship with India must take account of this extraordinary organisation.[2] By the time Hodges was working, the Company had become a powerful economic and political player there. And its influence was felt not just in Asia. The Company's commercial, political and military activities altered the way politicians and merchants in Britain thought about the wider world. Ultimately, it helped to lay the foundations of the British Raj. If the American colonies and Caribbean islands had once captured the British imagination, the commercial possibilities offered by the Indian subcontinent increasingly occupied British politicians, merchants and travellers as the eighteenth century neared its end.

But the 'intimate connection', as Hodges termed it, between India and Britain was not just a commercial or political one.[3] It was also an intensely visual one. The historian P. J. Marshall reminds us that the British encounter with India was 'prolonged and intense', and that it was concerned with cultural exchange as well as commercial endeavour and exploitation:

> Even by 1800, thousands of Englishmen had been to India, a huge flow of trade had developed (including the import of artefacts of high artistic quality), many books about India had been published in Britain and visual representations of India and Indians were being widely reproduced.[4]

James Rennell's much reprinted *Memoir of a Map of Hindoostan*, which first appeared in 1783, offers visual evidence of this (Fig. 1.2). It gave the public in Britain an image of India in which, as Rennell put it, 'no considerable blanks' remained.[5] It was a time, in other words, in which Europeans attempted to fill the linguistic, cultural and visual gaps in their knowledge of India. Images played a crucial part in this process. The visual variety of the subcontinent presented so many 'valuable subjects for the painter' that it attracted a host of artists and travellers keen to record, depict and bear witness.[6] Indeed, these artists helped to document and celebrate the richness and sophistication

Detail of Figure 1.4
Thomas Daniell and William Daniell, 'Calcutta from the River Hooghly: Gentoo Buildings', *Views of Calcutta*, 8, 1788

of Indian culture that later nineteenth-century views often denied. Artists contributed to the work of intellectual engagement with India, offering a parallel to activities in other disciplines such as cartography, comparative linguistics and topographical surveying. Like other European travellers and commentators, the British artists who depicted India in the period took their own expectations, preconceptions and prejudices with them, based on their artistic training, popular notions of taste and the prevailing political sentiments in Europe. Nevertheless these images, produced in the late eighteenth-century heyday of the East India Company, reflect its significance and the impact of its activities on Indians and Britons alike.

Among the artists who arrived on India's shores, Hodges was one of the most influential. He had served as the official expedition artist on James Cook's second voyage to the Pacific in 1772–5, and he exhibited regularly at the Free Society of Artists and the Royal Academy in London. His work offers some of the most striking insights into the ways in which British artists engaged with India, and we will encounter him

Figure 1.1
William Hodges,
'A View of the Fort of Agra', *Select Views in India, Drawn on the Spot, in the Years 1780, 1781, 1782, and 1783, and Executed in Aqua Tinta*, plate 15, 1785–88 (X 744(15))

and his work repeatedly in subsequent chapters. But he was not unique. This book charts the impact of India on a variety of British artists and travellers who, like Hodges, were fascinated by the sights and scenes before their eyes. And it also considers the impact of their work on audiences and viewers. While many aspects of the East India Company's story have been discussed by historians, few have considered the visual sources that survive and what they tell us about the connections between images and empire, pictures and power. This book draws on the unrivalled riches of the British Library – both visual and textual – to tell that history. It weaves together the story of individual images, their creators, and the people and events they depict. And, in doing so, it presents a detailed picture of the complex relationship between British artists and the people, places and cultures they encountered in India.

'A PERFECT PARADISE'

The attraction of India for artists was summed up by Ozias Humphry, who travelled to the subcontinent in the hope of finding artistic fame and worldly riches there: 'I think it is a blessed and glorious country, for the purpose we all visit it, and superior to any other upon earth.'[7] William Hodges described the sheer visual opulence that struck him as soon as he arrived at Madras:

> The clear, blue, cloudless sky, the polished white buildings, the bright sandy beach, and the dark green sea, present a combination totally new to the eye of the Englishman, just arrived from London, who, accustomed to the sight of the rolling masses of clouds floating in a damp atmosphere, cannot but contemplate the difference with delight: and the eye being thus gratified, the mind soon assumes a gay and tranquil habit, analogous to the pleasing objects with which it is surrounded.[8]

The eye of the artist was naturally drawn to the contrasts in colour and light that greeted Europeans in India. As we will see, Hodges and his colleagues did much to capture and convey this impression to their audiences in Europe. Indeed, Hodges had been recommended to Warren Hastings as someone desirous of recording 'the most curious appearances of nature and art in Asia'.[9] And he was equally charmed by Madras in the moonlight: 'Such a scene appears more like a tale of enchantment than a reality, to the imagination of a stranger just arrived.'[10] He found Bengal to be 'a perfect paradise'.[11] Elsewhere, the scenery assumed what James Forbes called 'a sublime aspect': 'the landscape is varied by stupendous heights, narrow glens, dark woods, and impenetrable jungles'.[12] And in *A Picturesque Tour along the Rivers Ganges and Jumna*, published in 1824, Charles Ramus Forrest wrote about the way in which he drew and coloured on the spot 'while the magic effects of the scenes represented were still impressed on his mental vision'. He hoped 'the reader will recollect with indulgence, that the colouring of the views, which so far exceeds that of the scenery of Europe, is but a just portrait of the enchanting features of India, eternally glowing in the brilliant glory of the resplendent Asiatic sun'.[13]

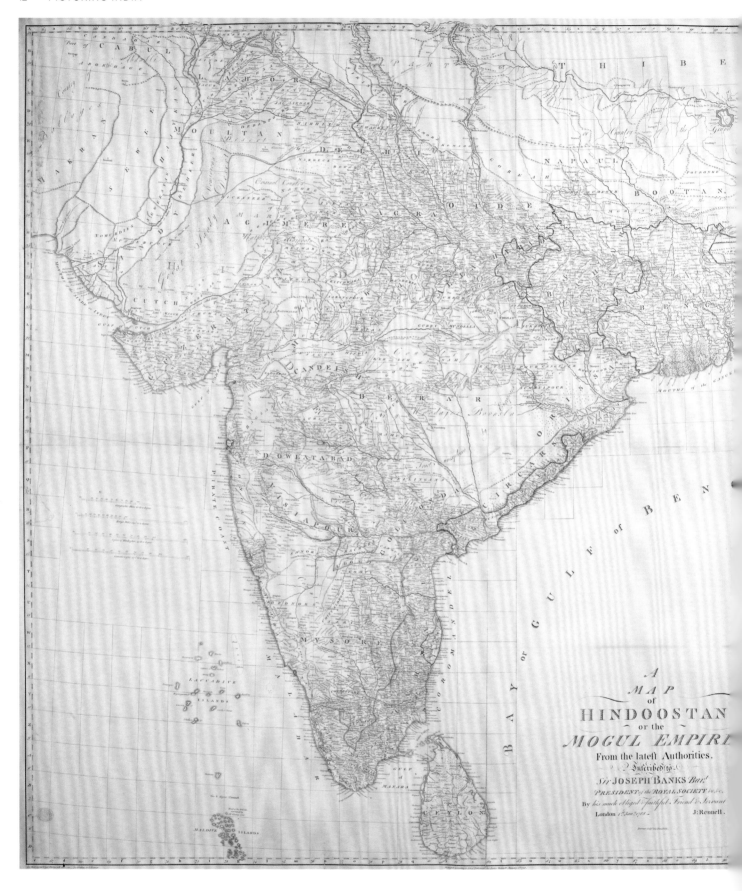

A
MAP
of
HINDOOSTAN
or the
MOGUL EMPIRE
From the latest Authorities.
Inscribed to
Sir JOSEPH BANKS Bart.
PRESIDENT of the ROYAL SOCIETY &c. &c.
By his much Obliged & faithful Friend & Servant
London 1st. Jan.ry 1788
J: Rennell.

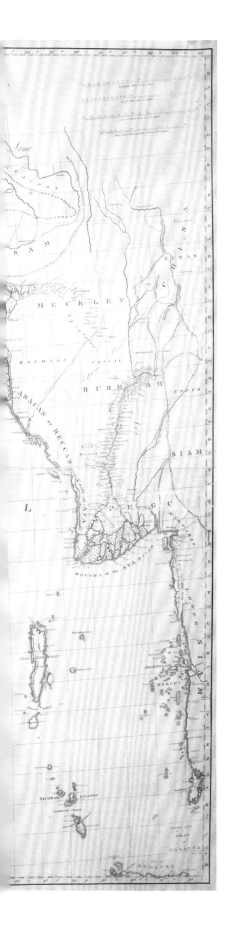

Figure 1.2
James Rennell,
'A Map of Hindoostan, or the Mogul Empire', 1783
(G.3014)

Some artists were undoubtedly also attracted by the wealth that they anticipated acquiring. According to one of his contemporaries, when he departed for India in 1783, Johan Zoffany fully expected 'to roll in gold dust'.[14] While Zoffany's sojourn in India was reasonably successful, not every artist found it equally lucrative or rewarding. Ozias Humphry ultimately set out on the advice of his friend, the engraver Sir Robert Strange. Sailing for Calcutta in 1785, Humphry was plagued by misfortune in India. His letters reveal anxieties about professional rivals as well as the hazards of business for a commercial artist working in the city. In April 1786 he complained to his brother in London that 'the times are not favourable for artists in India'.[15] He bemoaned his clients, European and Indian alike. Although he obtained a commission to paint the Nawab of Awadh and his courtiers at Lucknow in 1786, Humphry never received the fee of 47,000 rupees that was owed to him. And the climate took its toll on his health too. He arrived in Calcutta in November 1786, after eight months and a journey of nearly 3,000 miles upcountry, feeling that the climate had injured his health and damaged his eyesight. Ultimately, Humphry returned to London in 1787, a despondent and dejected figure. But others were more successful and revelled in the artistic inspiration they found all around them. For Thomas and William Daniell, their images were 'guiltless spoliations', apparently unconnected with a 'thirst for gold' or 'commercial speculations'.[16]

The story of Thomas Daniell and his nephew, William, gives a sense of how deeply intertwined the East India Company, the Indian subcontinent and its representation in visual images had become. The Daniells, like William Hodges, were instrumental in bringing India to audiences in Britain and making the country a subject for mainstream art there. One contemporary complimented the works of Thomas Daniell as 'increasing our enjoyment by bringing scenes to our fireside, too distant to visit, and too singular to be imagined'.[17] The influence of their work was extensive and enduring, and it can be seen in representations of India until the middle of the nineteenth century and beyond. Thomas Daniell was born near London in 1749. The son of an innkeeper, he was initially apprenticed to a coach builder. His artistic talents began to flourish when he worked for Charles Catton, coach painter to George III, between 1770 and 1773. Thomas subsequently enrolled in the Royal Academy Schools in 1773 and exhibited a number of pictures there over the next decade. However, his big break came when he received permission from the East India Company in 1784 to work as an 'engraver' in India. His nephew, William, travelled with him as his assistant and apprentice.

The Daniells worked primarily in Calcutta, the leading British commercial city in India by this time and one that, as we will see, was the basis for the Company's power in much of the rest of the country. There they restored paintings in the Council House and the Old Court House. They also produced the first topographical series of prints recording different scenes and prospects in this rapidly expanding commercial metropolis. Published as *Views of Calcutta* between 1786 and 1788, the twelve prints were engraved and coloured with the help of Indian artists. According to contemporary sources, they proved very popular among both Indian and European audiences. Claude Martin remarked that 'everybody has approved [their] Calcutta views'.[18] William Hodges thought that they offered excellent descriptions of 'the mixture of European

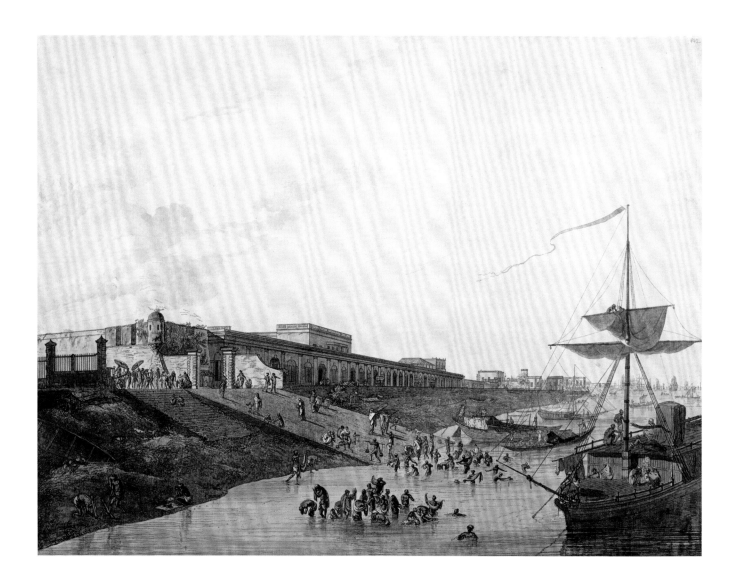

and Asiatic manners, which may be observed in Calcutta'. They also included scenes of daily life: 'coaches, phaetons, single horse chaises, with the pallankeens and hackeries of the natives – the passing ceremonies of the Hindoos – the different appearances of the fakirs – [which] form a sight perhaps more novel and extraordinary than any city in the world can present to a stranger.'[19] The Daniells captured the scenes of hustle and bustle in this thriving metropolis, translating the descriptions of travellers into visual images. For example, Thomas Twining's account of the scene that met him on arriving at Calcutta in 1792 found visual expression in 'The Old Fort, Ghaut', the sixth print in the Daniells' series (Fig. 1.3):

Figure 1.3
Thomas Daniell and William Daniell,
'The Old Fort, Ghaut', *Views of Calcutta*, plate 6,
1787 (P92)

Figure 1.4
Thomas Daniell and William Daniell,
'Calcutta from the River Hooghly:
Gentoo Buildings', *Views of Calcutta*, plate 8,
1788 (P47)

I quitted the boat at a spacious sloping ghaut or landing-place, close to the north-west angle of the old fort. The lower slope went some way into the water, and was crowded with natives, men and women, bathing with their clothes, or rather cloths on, and which they dexterously contrived to change under water, without embarrassment to themselves or the bystanders.[20]

Their view of 'Calcutta from the River Hooghly' conveyed a similarly lively scene with the crowded river bustling with all sorts of craft (Fig. 1.4). In the centre is a pinnace budgerow, of the type used by the Daniells themselves, flying a Union flag. So-called 'country boats', or indigenous craft, with bamboo decks and great rudders can be seen all around, and a horse-headed pleasure craft is also visible. Meanwhile the shore is lined with the houses and warehouses on which the commercial success of the city depended. Scenes like these, captured and conveyed so powerfully in the graphic work of these artists, played a big part in making the Company's commercial and political activity in India – half the world away from Britain – a reality for viewers.

But it was not only in the commercial heart of East India Company power in the subcontinent that British artists worked. Just as Hodges travelled extensively, so too did the Daniells play a vital role in visually documenting a wide geographical and cultural range of sites across India. In fact, they travelled more than any of their contemporaries, earning the title 'artist-adventurers'. The Daniells made three tours: a trip from Calcutta to Srinagar (1788–91), a circular tour from Mysore to Madras (1792–3) and a visit to Bombay and its temple sites (1793). They sketched, drew and painted as they travelled. On returning to Calcutta after their first expedition, the uncle and nephew team produced 150 oil paintings, which they sold by public lottery. As well as spreading visual information about the country among British residents in Bengal, their efforts also enabled them to finance a second tour, to Mysore in southern India. This region had recently been the scene of an intense battle for political dominance, played out between Hyder Ali and his son, Tipu Sultan, and the East India Company. A second lottery, comprising sixty-eight oil paintings and eight drawings, was drawn in Madras in February 1793. This funded their third and final tour. On this occasion, the Daniells travelled to western India. Throughout their time in India, and in addition to recording the landscapes and people that they encountered, they also restored and completed pictures for Europeans, experimented with copperplate engraving and occasionally made pencil portrait sketches.

Like many of the artists discussed in this book, the impact and importance of the Daniells' work was not confined to India. It also made a lasting impression back in Britain. Indeed, the work of these 'two artists of splendid talents' was seen in Britain long before they returned from India. In 1788, for example, William Hickey entrusted 'a present for my brother' to Philip Yonge, a barrister returning to Europe for the sake of his health: 'twelve views of different parts of Calcutta, drawn and engraved in *aqua tinta* by Messrs Daniell'.[21] The Daniells returned to London in September 1794, where they began to make use of the hundreds of drawings and sketches that they had taken in India, working them up into watercolours, prints and finished oil paintings. Their output was astonishing. Every year between 1795 and 1838, one or other of them exhibited pictures at the Royal Academy and the British Institution, important venues for the display of art in London. They also embarked on a vast project and spent the next thirteen years making 144 aquatints for a publication entitled *Oriental Scenery*. This work was published in six parts between 1795 and 1808 and cost a colossal £210 a set. Uncle and nephew engraved all the plates themselves and probably did some of the colouring too. One of the most comprehensive records of Indian life at the time, the prints represent Mughal and Dravidian (southern Indian) architecture and monuments, cityscapes and sublime views of mountains and waterfalls. *Oriental*

Figure 1.5
Gangaram Chintaman Tambat,
Gungarum, 1790s (YCBA, B1977.14.22249)

Figure 1.6
Indian artist, *A Bookbinder*, 1798–1804
(Add. Or. 1111)

Scenery represents the most extensive work of its kind, and it attracted subscribers throughout Britain, as well as in Calcutta and Madras. William Daniell later confessed that for seven years after he returned from India he worked daily from six in the morning until midnight. And they did not stop here. In 1810 they published *A Picturesque Voyage to India by the Way of China*, and over the years they also produced many single plates for publications, such as the *Oriental Annual*. But it was *Oriental Scenery* that acted as the ultimate guide for future artistic travellers wanting to follow in their footsteps. Its large-scale format, the number of plates and the use of colour printing were greatly admired and emulated by those who saw them. Little wonder then that when William Simpson was commissioned to go to India to make drawings for a series of 250 lithographs for Day and Son – to record scenes of the great tumult there in the late 1850s – he prepared by looking at images in the India Office Library made by Hodges and the Daniells.

It was not just professional European artists – like the Daniells or William Hodges – who helped to broker the relationship with India and bring scenes of Indian life and landscapes to the attention of British viewers. East India Company officials were often keen on employing local Indian artists. The Maratha artist Gangaram Chintaman Tambat, for example, compiled an album of sketches and drawings for Charles Warre Malet of the Bombay Civil Service (Fig. 1.5). Gangaram was probably trained at the drawing academy established by the Maratha Peshwa at his court in Poona. Similarly, the 'Wellesley Album' (see Chapter 5), now in the collection of the India Office, consists of some 138 drawings depicting monuments, manners and customs which were almost certainly done by Indian artists working in Calcutta in the 1790s (Fig. 1.6).

It is also important to remember that much of the visual recording of India was undertaken by amateurs: only about 10 per cent of the visual material in the collection of the India Office was done by professional artists. Amateurs had to work without the extensive classical training, encouragement and patronage enjoyed by their professional peers. East India Company military officers were taught drawing at Addiscombe, the Company's military college, as part of their general training. But it only offered a basic introduction and, when they got to India, few amateurs had access to professional artists for advice and support. James Forbes, for example, arrived as a sixteen-year-old in 1765 and recalled his predicament: 'India was formerly not the resort of artists; when there I had little to excite emulation, and no other instruction than a few friendly hints from Sir Archibald Campbell; who, during a short residence at Bombay … encouraged my juvenile [artistic] pursuits.'[22] And all of these artists – amateur and professional, Asian and European – had to overcome the climate, the danger of disease, and the difficult terrain and travelling conditions to make a remarkable record of the East India Company and British engagement with India.

IMAGES AND EMPIRE

The work of these artists helped to make visual sense of a country that would become a jewel in the crown of Britain's Victorian empire. As well as providing a record of time and travels in India, and the sheer visual delight these places evoked in those who

Figure 1.7
John McClean
'Ruins of the Citadel in Pondicherry
after the Attack by the British', 1762
(WD1293)

documented them, the images produced by travelling, professional and amateur artists also reveal a great deal about the conditions and contexts in which they were created.

A simple pen, ink and wash drawing by an amateur artist, John McClean, suggests some of the ways in which images can illuminate our understanding of the British engagement with India in the period (Fig. 1.7). McClean was a military man. He had travelled to India in 1762 as an ensign in the Madras Engineers. His faculty in visual recording probably derives from this training rather than from any artistic ambitions. But his image of the citadel in Pondicherry introduces many of the ideas and motifs that characterise the depiction of India by other British artists at the time. One of the most intriguing aspects is the artist's inclusion of himself in the image. McClean depicted himself sketching in the foreground. This operates as a kind of visual guarantee of authenticity, reassuring the viewer of the truthfulness of the image by placing its creator in a prominent position. Accuracy was valued and its achievement frequently underlined. Many of the artists who travelled in the subcontinent were at pains to point out how objective their visual records were, and how they reinforced, and even surpassed, the textual and written accounts. William Hodges is a case in point. The remarks that he made on his travels represented 'a few plain observations, noted down upon the spot, in the simple garb of truth, without the smallest embellishment from fiction, or from fancy'. And he continued: 'The drawings, from which the plates for this work are engraved, I have already mentioned were made upon the spot; and, to the utmost of my ability, are fair and accurate representations of the original.'[23] Nevertheless, they were still the products of their time, where aesthetic considerations and artistic training worked together to influence the way in which views were produced.

At first glance, then, this might appear to be a completely objective record of the scene. But McClean's image might also have symbolic resonances: viewers would have been aware that drawing or contemplating the ruins of fallen empires was an evocative theme, laden with ideas about the transience of life and the fleeting nature of all human endeavour. Jemima Kindersley, one of the first British women to publish her experiences of travel in India, remarked on the 'ruinous' surroundings of Pondicherry in June 1765. The city 'fills me with a sort of pleasing melancholy; one feels a kind of reverence and pity for ruined grandeur, even in things inanimate: a small part of the palace remains standing, but not more than two houses in the whole town. And those, as well as the noble fortifications, [are] in a shattered condition.'[24]

Finally, the context in which the image was produced is also important. Quite apart from any symbolism or artistic licence employed in its creation, the image records a key moment in the East India Company's rise to power in India. Pondicherry was a French trading fort on the east coast that was captured by the British during the Seven Years War, a global struggle between the two emerging superpowers. British victories in North America and the Caribbean, as well as in the seas off Europe, were vital in winning the war. But the parallel successes of British arms in India helped to propel the East India Company to its dominant position in the subcontinent. Sir Eyre Coote, who led the assault on Pondicherry, had already steered his troops to victory over the French at Wandiwash and Arcot before they laid siege to Pondicherry. After

Figure 1.8
John Johnson,
*Waterfall near Haliyal with Johnson
Sketching in the Foreground*, 1801
(WD1055, f. 32)

a blockade lasting some eight months, the French finally surrendered on 16 January 1761. McClean's image captures the aftermath of the devastating siege. Although his career in the subcontinent was sadly short-lived – he died near Madras in February 1768 – this image encapsulates many of the intertwined themes of art and empire that we will explore throughout this book.

Similar themes can be found in a watercolour painted nearly forty years later by Captain John Johnson of the Bombay Engineers (Fig. 1.8). Like McClean, Johnson also represented himself in the foreground of the image, underlining his role as a reliable eyewitness of the scene laid out before him and us. This image was also made in the aftermath of a British military victory, created shortly after the British had finally defeated Tipu Sultan, the ruler of Mysore and one of the most tenacious opponents of British rule in the subcontinent. That conflict attracted considerable artistic attention: the Daniells, as we have seen, travelled to Mysore in the 1790s to gather inspiration and make records. Others prepared large canvases on the subject for exhibition in Britain. But Johnson was not a professional artist. And, unlike McClean's depiction of rubble and ruins, there is little evidence of the extensive and intense fighting. A tree forms a natural visual bracket for the waterfall that occupies the main focus of the scene. And, yet, the visual charm of the image needs to be seen in the context of Johnson's role as an engineer, charged with constructing the kinds of engineering projects and military surveillance that formed part of his everyday work and that helped to defeat Tipu and his troops. Aesthetic considerations and artistic composition undoubtedly played a role in creating all of these images, but they sit side by side with the unfolding drama of the Company's rise to power in India.

ART AND BRITISH INDIA

The expansion of the East India Company's activities in the subcontinent and the number of permanent British residents there created a market for pictures within India. The success of the Daniells, mainly among the small European resident community, bears out this point. But, as early as 1770, Baron Carl von Imhoff, the first husband of Warren Hastings's wife Marian, remarked on how profitable painting was in Calcutta. People were, apparently, willing to pay huge prices.[25] When Catherine Read arrived in Calcutta in 1777, her prospects looked promising. In February 1778 Major Kyd was 'confident (not in my own opinion alone, but on Mrs Hastings's also) that you will have every reason to be satisfied in point of emolument from the exercises of paint-ing' in Calcutta.[26] As Britain's ties with India deepened, the number of artists there expanded exponentially: in 1792 Gavin Hamilton in Calcutta mentioned Robert Home, Arthur William Devis, John Alefounder, Frans Balthazar Solvyns, as well as Thomas and William Daniell.[27] The following year, William Baillie, another of Ozias Humphry's artistic contacts in India, wrote about many of the same people, adding news of Mrs Hill, John Smart and Mrs Baxter.[28]

But many of these artists were not only interested in appealing to Indian residents. They wanted to sell their works to audiences in Britain too. As a result, representa-tions of India by artists who had been there became an equally powerful force in shaping British perceptions of the region. There was certainly a popular appetite for such descriptions and depictions in Europe. James Rennell, writing in 1788, remarked that 'almost every particular relating to Hindoostan is become an object of popular curiosity' in Britain.[29] On some occasions, the images were produced, exhibited and sold in Britain. But they were also sent directly from India. Benjamin Mee, a financier in Calcutta, introduced depictions of India to European viewers by sending views by 'Mr Daniel' to his sister and brother-in-law back in England.[30] These images, and their visual impact, had effects elsewhere in Europe. The great traveller Alexander von Humboldt maintained that Hodges's Indian views had encouraged him to travel. He credited seeing 'paintings by Hodge [sic] in the house of Warren Hastings in London, representing the banks of the Ganges' as one of the youthful experiences that 'awakened … the first beginnings of an inextinguishable longing to visit the tropics'.[31]

The example of William Hodges is instructive, as his work had a profound impact on the way European audiences came to regard India. Hodges exhibited twenty-five paintings at the Royal Academy between 1785 and 1794: he exhibited eight Indian landscapes at the Royal Academy exhibition of 1786 alone. Forty-eight aquatints – a type of etching that produced finished prints that resembled watercolours – were published between 1785 and 1788 in his *Select Views in India*, and fourteen engravings based on paintings and drawings illustrated his book, *Travels in India* (1793). The final bound volume of *Select Views* covered the entire range of Hodges's experience in India. The prints were often hand-coloured by Hodges himself, and they represent the kind of high-quality, prestigious commercial venture designed to appeal to the rising interest in India in Britain. The images frequently show sites that refer to recent events associated with the British in India, particularly military successes. Taken together, the prints in Hodges's *Select Views* offer a very positive interpretation of the East India Company and its activities in India.

Hodges and the Daniells exhibited their work at grand art exhibitions in London. But they were joined by many other artists whom we shall encounter below. For example, Francis Swain Ward, who had gone to India in 1757 as a lieutenant, exhibited Indian landscapes at the Society of Artists between 1765 and 1773. And it was not just at the heart of artistic society that representations of the subcontinent appeared. Indian pictures appeared in as many as 20 per cent of all the house sales managed by Christie's. The market in prints and illustrated books also helped to foster an interest among wealthy readers in Europe. As we have seen, the six volumes of Thomas and William Daniell's *Oriental Scenery*, published between 1795 and 1808, conveyed images of the subcontinent to a wide British public. Using prints was a common route for artists seeking a broader audience and a wider appeal for their work. Thomas Longcroft, a young artist who lived with Zoffany in India, sent home drawings to be engraved, according to Gavin Hamilton.[32] James Forbes's *Oriental Memoirs* (1813), Captain Thomas Williamson's *Oriental Field Sports* (1819), Charles D'Oyly's *Costumes of India* (1830) and Emily Eden's *Portraits of the Princes and Peoples of India* (1844) indicate the continued popularity of images and texts in presenting the British engagement with India in the early nineteenth century.

Images charting the rise of the Company's power and the increasing British engagement with the subcontinent circulated in a number of other contexts too. In many cases, the artists responsible had never been to India or witnessed the scenes or events being depicted. But the public interest demonstrates the popular fascination with the subcontinent and British exploits there. For example, Francis Hayman painted four canvases to adorn the annexe of the Rotunda at the Vauxhall Pleasure Gardens in 1762, one of which depicted Lord Clive meeting Mir Jafar after the Battle of Plassey, an event which heralded the beginnings of Company control in India. A few decades later, the fall of Tipu Sultan in 1799 inspired much visual as well as political interest in Britain. Popular panoramas, history paintings depicting Tipu's death, a profusion of prints, and popular exhibitions contributed to this phenomenon. Robert Ker Porter capitalised on the public fascination by painting a 120-foot-long panorama in just six weeks. Depicted on a semi-circular plane, the *Storming of Seringapatam* was a pictorial reconstruction of the fourth Anglo-Mysore War. When it went on display at the Lyceum Theatre, on the Strand, it transported viewers to the scene. One contemporary, Thomas Frognall Dibdin, commented that 'you seemed to be listening to the groans of the wounded and the dying', whose 'red hot blood' was spilled all over the canvas. The realism of the scene produced 'a sight that was altogether as marvellous as it was novel. You carried it home, and did nothing but think of it, talk of it, and dream of it.'[33] India inspired the compilation of a vast and diverse corpus of visual material.

PICTURING INDIA

One of the strongest themes running through this book, then, is the sheer visual impact of India, its people and places on British artists. In addition to its extensive commercial and political activities, the East India Company nurtured the careers of professional artists like William Hodges, Johan Zoffany, and Thomas and William Daniell. European artists painted the Company's new possessions, portrayed its servants and decorated its headquarters in London. Their work brought British audiences face to face with strange places and unfamiliar scenes. By exploring the extraordinary body of visual evidence created by these events, *Picturing India* sketches out the transformation of the East India Company from trader to sovereign in the space of a few decades.

The following chapters represent crucial aspects of Britain's engagement with the subcontinent in the late eighteenth and early nineteenth centuries, and the ways in which they were depicted in images. Visual records of the Company's activities in India testify to shifting British attitudes towards the wider world, as well as to the power of images to preserve and convey momentous political and social changes. But these images also record the excitement and wonder of their creators in the face of natural beauty, as well as preserving and expressing the human interactions and encounters at the heart of the story. In their breadth and variety, then, the images in this book and the stories associated with them illustrate the capacity of art to reflect the complex nuances of Britain's relationship with the subcontinent in the period.

Chapter 2 introduces the story of the Company and the broader historical context of its rise from a trading enterprise to a territorial power. It charts the geographical extent of the Company's operations, its maritime connections and the places where its ships called. In doing so, it suggests the role that images played in presenting the evolving story of the Company to the viewing public. The discussion pays particular attention to those ports on the coast of India that were so vital to the East India Company's trading world. The Company's power was intimately entwined with these coastal cities, where early Company endeavours established tenuous footholds only with the blessing and help of local Indian rulers. Soon, however, these 'factories' became bridgeheads, facilitating greater expansion and commercial penetration into the interior. By the middle of the eighteenth century, the landscapes of India were opening to the British gaze.

In their explorations of the people and places that defined the Company's engagement with India, Chapters 3 and 4 are especially rich in visual images. At the heart of this story was a profound visual interest in the landscapes of India. The long-established themes and tropes of landscape scenery as it was seen in Europe – beautiful, picturesque and sublime by turn – were transferred to the subcontinent. And the artists who came to depict these scenes were increasingly of the first rank: professional, influential and well connected. But if places in India attracted artistic attention, so too did the people associated with East India Company rule there. Company men – officials and soldiers, governors and generals – were depicted by artists keen to earn professional respect and financial rewards, using the time-honoured traditions of portrait painting. But there is also a small band of Indians, from all ranks of life, whose images adorn the Company's archives. In all of these portraits, the stance, gestures and expressions of the sitter, together with the accoutrements and objects surrounding them, offer a carefully constructed image of these individuals and their role in the Company's world.

All of these artistic representations need to be seen, of course, in the context of this private trading company whose control became so powerful and ultimately corrosive. Chapter 5 brings the discussion back to Britain, exploring some of the ways in which the patronage of art by the East India Company and its officials brought views of India into circulation in Britain. The commissioning of a portrait by a Company official for his country house and the purchase of a set of prints were just some of the ways in which the Company and its activities influenced art in Britain. This chapter also considers the Company's crucial role as a patron of art and conveyor of information about India in its own right. The Company's commissions for its London headquarters offer an ideal lens through which to view the way in which art and architecture worked to define financial might, commercial wealth and political power. By investigating the visual language of the Company's headquarters, this chapter suggests that East India House, in Leadenhall Street at the heart of the City of London, acted as a visual symbol of the Company's power and prestige. But, in order to understand the origins of that power and prestige, we need to return to India and to assess the Company's involvement in power politics and port cities in the subcontinent.

CHAPTER 2

Politics, power and port cities

On 23 June 1757 Robert Clive, a former East India Company clerk, led a small group of men to victory at the Battle of Plassey in north-eastern India. Clive triumphed more by political intrigue than military might, cutting deals with his opponent's internal enemies to ensure that his 3,000-strong force was not overwhelmed in battle. No matter how it was achieved, however, Plassey was a momentous event. It established the East India Company as a significant player in northern India and ushered in a new era in British relations with the entire region. Victory at Plassey consolidated the power of a private trading concern – the London-based East India Company – and heralded the beginnings of that company's century-long role as a major political force in India. It became, in the words of Edmund Burke, 'a state in the guise of a merchant, a great public office in the disguise of a counting-house'.[1] In doing so, it laid the foundations for Britain's Indian Raj, which would last until the middle of the twentieth century. This chapter introduces the history of the Company's involvement in India, the political machinations that led to its transformation into a territorial empire, and the economic and geographical parameters that provided the framework for all British artistic engagement with the subcontinent. The travellers, amateur draughtsmen and professional artists who chronicled their impressions and made visual records of India in the later eighteenth century did so against the backdrop of the Company's relationship with India. And it is impossible to appreciate these images – or to offer potential interpretations of them – without understanding something of the wider political context in which these landscapes, cityscapes and portraits were being created.

As with much of the Company's history, the background and wider context of the Battle of Plassey are complex and deeply entwined with a range of local and global circumstances. Historians are still debating its impact and legacy. But contemporaries were unequivocal. They regarded it as bringing about a 'revolution', which established Company, and by extension British, political mastery over the nawabs, or rulers, of Bengal and their territory. The *London Magazine* published an extensive report because it was concerned that 'an action of such éclat is not sufficiently known to the generality of people, here at home'. Readers were informed that Clive's actions at Palashi (anglicised as 'Plassey'), a small village some ninety miles north of Calcutta, 'gloriously and successfully closed' his earlier endeavours in southern India. The written report was accompanied by a visual plan of the action (Fig. 2.1). It was, readers were assured, 'a very accurate and authentic one'.[2] The yoking together of text and image here reminds us of the varied and vital role played by visual records in explaining the consolidation of Company power and Britain's developing relationship with India. And these images were not just confined to sketch maps or topographical drawings done in the field. The Company's growing power, as a result of Plassey, was also expressed through more elevated and sophisticated artistic creations.

Benjamin West's epic painting showing *Shah Alam II Conveying the Grant of the Diwani to Lord Clive* is one example of the way in which a successful, well-connected professional artist in Britain engaged with the evolving story of the Company in India (Fig. 2.2). West was president of the Royal Academy for a time, and his enormous canvas evokes one of the most important legacies of the Battle of Plassey and one of

Detail of Figure 2.3
Spiridione Roma,
The East Offering its Riches to Britannia,
1778 (F245)

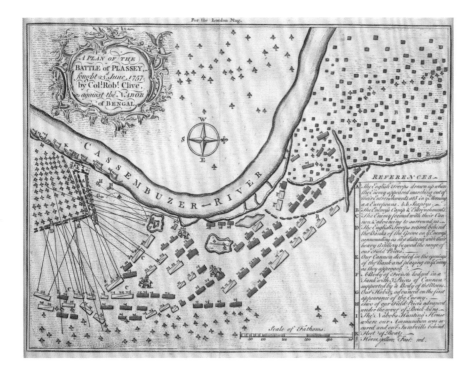

Figure 2.1
'Plan of the Battle of Plassey, Fought 23 June 1757 by Col. Robert Clive, against the Nabob of Bengal', published in the *London Magazine*, January 1760 (P1437)

the most crucial events in the history of the British Empire. The carefully constructed composition and the deliberate gestures of the protagonists only hint at the import of the occasion. Far more than the fighting in Bengal, the event depicted by West represents the genesis of Company control in India. In conveying the *diwani*, the Mughal emperor, Shah Alam, installed the London-based Company as his representatives in the wealthy and populous province of Bengal, with the right to collect taxes and administer justice. The Company had become a state in all but name: the piece of paper that forms the focus of the painting's composition was effectively its founding charter as a territorial power.

Only a few decades later, the Company's transformation was given further visual expression in its headquarters in the City of London. East India House presented a visual feast for visitors and employees alike. One of the treasures on display, Spiridione Roma's *The East Offering its Riches to Britannia*, encapsulated some of the results that flowed from the event depicted by West (Fig. 2.3). Little is known of this Greek artist who came to England in 1770. He was employed at The Vyne in Hampshire by its owner, John Chute, who subsequently dismissed him for 'being idle'. By 1778, Roma was in London where the Company commissioned him to paint a piece to adorn the ceiling of the Revenue Committee Room in East India House, one of the most important spaces in the entire building. The painting presents personifications rather than depicting real, historical individuals. It was designed to be interpreted symbolically,

Figure 2.2
Benjamin West,
*Shah Alam II Conveying the Grant of the
Diwani to Lord Clive*, c. 1818 (F29)

Figure 2.3
Spiridione Roma,
The East Offering its Riches to Britannia, 1778
(F245)

with each element carefully selected and articulated to add to the overall impression of a successful commercial organisation. An article published in the *Gentleman's Magazine* of 1778 pointed out that Britannia, sitting securely on a rock or pedestal, signified the Company's stability. A river-god, apparently representing the Ganges, pours water out at Britannia's feet. Meanwhile, Mercury, the god of merchandise, presents various Eastern lands to her. The figure representing Persia is shown with silks and spices, that for China with tea and porcelain and that for India with pearls and jewels. In the distance, a ship is under sail. It is flying the distinctive ensign of the Company: parallel horizontal red and white stripes with the flag of St George in the canton. The vessel acts as 'an emblem of that commerce from which both Britannia and the Company derive great and singular advantages'.[3] The overarching message is unmistakeable: the people of Asia are offering a cornucopia of riches to Britannia through her representative, the East India Company. Here was a company thriving on its maritime might, political power and commercial accomplishments.

Although these images are very different in terms of content, intended location and prospective audience, they are linked. In their visual vocabulary, as well as their subject matter, they capture something of the East India Company's rise to power in the second half of the eighteenth century. All of this political power was directed to consolidating and increasing the Company's maritime trade. This chapter begins by outlining the background to the Company's position in mid-eighteenth-century India, putting the Battle of Plassey and some of its consequences in context. It considers some of the ways in which these were presented in visual images. The second half of the chapter introduces the maritime context of the Company's activities, exploring the ships, the maritime trade routes along which they travelled and the port cities at which they called. It explores their depiction in a variety of images and texts, suggesting the central role played by sea ports and coastal cities in the Company's trading empire.

THE ORIGINS OF A TRADING EMPIRE

The East India Company was established on 31 December 1600. On this day, the Company was awarded a trading charter by the Privy Council of Queen Elizabeth. This charter gave the small group of 218 merchants, who had come together to form the company, a monopoly on English trade with Asia for fifteen years. (After the Act of Union in 1707, its monopoly covered all British trade to Asia.) The charter granted concessions on customs payments and allowed the Company to export bullion. But everything else was the responsibility of the Company itself. Soon after its first forays into Asian trade, it became a joint-stock company, an arrangement which allowed its members to pool their resources and ensured continuity in the Company's business activities. Although its early years were difficult, the Company was here to stay. By the middle of the seventeenth century, it had some 1500 shareholders, and by the end of the eighteenth century this number had doubled. Merchants always constituted the bulk of the investors but the Company also attracted interest from nobility, gentry, professionals and a number of foreign investors. These shareholders formed what came to be known as the General Court of the Company. The day-to-day running of the Company was carried out by the Court of Directors, which was elected annually and consisted of substantial businessmen as well as people who had returned from India. Under their governor or chairman, the twenty-four directors usually met once a week or more. As the charter was renewable at intervals, the Company needed to cultivate close and friendly relations with government ministers and other politicians. By the middle of the eighteenth century, therefore, the Company had a long track record of brokering Britain's relationship with Asia.

With a monopoly on all British trade east of the Cape of Good Hope, the Company's geographical interests and commercial catchment area were necessarily broad. It began by concentrating its commercial activities on South-East Asia – the location of the famed Spice Islands – where it traded for a range of rare and expensive spices, such as pepper, nutmeg and mace. It also tried to cultivate connections with China, the only source of lucrative commodities like tea and porcelain in the eighteenth century. But, even by the end of the seventeenth century, India was the primary focus of the Company's political and commercial undertakings. Some Company men urged it to adopt an aggressive empire-building approach to its operations there. One of these was Sir Josiah Child, who had ambitious plans for increasing the population and expanding the trade of the Company's Indian settlements. Child worried that, as long as they continued 'in the state of meer [sic] merchants', the Company and its servants were always liable 'to be turned out at the pleasure of the Dutch and abused at the discretion of the natives'.[4] He encouraged the Company's servants in India to use force to obtain trade concessions. In Child's day, this policy led to a disastrously unsuccessful war against the Mughal emperor, Aurangzeb, in western India and in

Figure 2.4
Francis Swain Ward,
*The Rock at Trichinopoly, Madras,
with the Barracks*, 1772–73 (F24)

Bengal in 1689. But Child's advice anticipated the approach that would lead to such astonishing expansion in the century that followed.

When the Company's ships first called at Indian ports, the subcontinent was a complicated patchwork of independent kingdoms, principalities and states, many of which came under the ultimate authority of the Mughal emperor in Delhi. By the middle of the eighteenth century, however, a tottering Mughal Empire, combined with rising international tension and rivalry with the French, encouraged the Company to take a more proactive role in Indian affairs. At the heart of the Company's rise to prominence in India was its increasing involvement in local politics. An example of this can be seen in southern India, where the death of the Nizam of Hyderabad in 1748 prompted a struggle over succession rights, with the British and French supporting rival claimants to the throne. Eventually, Muhammed Ali Khan Walla Jah, backed by British power, succeeded in becoming Nawab of the Carnatic (sometimes called the Nawab of Arcot after the major town in his dominions). He seized the great rock fortress at Trichinopoly (today's Tiruchirappalli), which dominated the valley of the river Kaveri and controlled the irrigation channels watering the paddy lands of Trichinopoly and Tanjore. The rock had been a place of human settlement from prehistoric times and, in subsequent centuries, it had become a sacred site for both Hindus and Muslims. In the middle of the eighteenth century, however, the fortress was at the centre of a global and regional tussle for power, with the French laying siege to it. Little wonder, then, that it should have been such a focus for Francis Swain Ward, who depicted its massive bulk in an oil painting based on drawings and sketches taken during his travels in the region in the early 1760s (Fig. 2.4). Eventually, Robert Clive and Stringer Lawrence moved against Trichinopoly, raised the siege, outmanoeuvred the besiegers and ultimately denied the French their much-sought supremacy in southern India. In doing so, Clive and Lawrence paved the way for the introduction of Company control there, which was established when the Peace of Paris brought the Seven Years War to an end in 1763. It is little wonder, then, that this reminder of another remarkable landmark in the story of the Company's growing authority, and a suitably stark example of its achievements, should adorn East India House, where Ward's painting hung in the Committee of Correspondence's meeting room.

The success of Clive and Lawrence in southern India was the prelude to greater triumphs further north. Almost immediately upon seeing off the threat of the French and their allies in the south, Clive was on his way to sort out an even more problematic situation in Bengal, in the north-east of the subcontinent. Here the young Nawab, Siraj-ud-Daulah, was trying to re-establish his authority and power in the region. The British East India Company, along with cartels of Indian financiers and regional landholders, was one of the institutions targeted by the Nawab. His armies occupied Calcutta, leading to the infamous 'Black Hole' incident. However, Clive's expeditionary force recaptured Calcutta in January 1757 and, on 23 June 1757, defeated the Nawab's armies at the Battle of Plassey. Clive had done a secret deal with the Nawab's internal enemies at his court. The dissident commander-in-chief, Mir Jafar, was installed as the new nawab. He was, in theory at least, an independent ally of the Company. In

practice, the Company maintained a large army that assumed responsibility for the defence of Bengal and insisted on payments from the new Nawab for its services, thus quickly eroding his autonomy. In 1760 a coup engineered by the British brought down Mir Jafar and replaced him with yet another nawab, Mir Kasim. The commercial and political power of the Company expanded in the years that followed. Mir Kasim, in turn, was driven out of Bengal and he and his allies were defeated by Company forces at the Battle of Buxar in 1764. The subsequent Treaty of Allahabad, signed on 12 August 1765, appointed the East India Company as the Diwan (or chief financial manager) of the provinces of Bengal, Bihar and Orissa. This was the culmination of nearly a decade of politicking in Bengal and, as we have seen, it was celebrated in West's enormous canvas. What essentially amounted to the right to collect revenue in these provinces was usually assessed as being worth around the equivalent of £2 million per annum to the Company.

By 1772, and in light of these developments, Bengal was effectively a Company territory. The responsibility for defending the province and maintaining law and order were also partly dependent on the Company as the Nawab's army had been disbanded, leaving him with little power to implement any decision that was not acceptable to the Company. The British Empire in India had truly begun. The Company's ultimate success put it in a position of power which it would maintain for nearly a century.

Figure 2.5
Delhi School,
Panorama of a Durbar Procession of Akbar II, Emperor of Delhi, probably at Id or after Ramadan, c. 1815 (Add. Or. 888)

But it also heralded the beginnings of a deeper artistic and visual engagement with the subcontinent. As we have seen, these extraordinary events were reflected in the vogue for dramatic paintings of historical events and key landmarks. In addition to the works created by West, Ward and Roma, which were aimed primarily at a knowledgeable audience closely associated with the Company, the impact of these political developments stretched far beyond East India House. For example, Francis Hayman, a well-known and accomplished society artist, depicted the aftermath of the Battle of Plassey in a painting destined for a prime viewing location at the heart of the Vauxhall Pleasure Gardens. Hayman's picture was seen by thousands of visitors who flocked to this fashionable venue, and it became one of the earliest and most widely viewed depictions of Anglo-Indian history in this new phase of East India Company dominance.

Under the governor-generalship of Warren Hastings, from 1772, the Company's influence and territories expanded even further. Hastings was fully aware that Bengal, in its 'extent ... and its possible resources', was 'equal to those of most states in Europe'.[5] Its population numbered some 20 million people, its public revenue amounted to about a quarter of that of Britain itself, it maintained an army of approximately 25,000 men, it had its own foreign policy for dealings with other Indian states, and the value of its exports to Britain was rising towards £1 million a year. As before, the Company's ability to master Indian diplomacy and navigate the treacherous shoals of Indian politics was key to its success. Hastings sought to maintain British influence by creating and managing a complex system of alliances. British agents were posted as residents at Indian courts, Indian rulers were encouraged to sign treaties, and they were forced to accept garrisons of British troops, for which they paid heavy subsidies. For example, under the guise of maintaining alliances, rulers such as the nawabs of Awadh and Arcot paid huge sums of 'protection money' to the East India Company, which stationed troops on their territory.

We get an impression of the complex and intricate politics of the subcontinent – as well as of the importance of hierarchy and diplomacy – in the representation of durbars. These were ceremonies or public receptions in which the local ruler conspicuously displayed his power and influence to the general population. The tradition was famously adopted and adapted by later British administrations but it built on long-standing and well-established local practices. Durbars gave Indian and European artists alike the opportunity to record a visual spectacle and to reflect the complex political power dynamics in imagery. An example of this can be seen in a watercolour of the durbar procession of Akbar II in Delhi, painted by an Indian artist around 1815 (Fig. 2.5). Although the British controlled the city by 1803, the authority of the Mughal emperor still applied within the walls of the Red Fort. As a result, the representatives of the East India Company continued to pay formal respect to the emperor. British officials played a secondary role in the great royal festivals and processions which, on the surface at least, confirmed Mughal authority. A similar pattern of display was also evident in the south. A watercolour by George Chinnery, showing a durbar at Madras on 18 February 1805, depicts Major-General Arthur Wellesley being received at the Chepauk Palace by Azim al-Daula, the Nawab of the Carnatic (Fig. 2.6). Wellesley, the future Duke of Wellington, is introduced by Lord William Cavendish Bentinck, the Governor of Madras. Both of the British officers are standing in front of the Nawab, who is seated on his *masnad*. Although both of these images derive from the early nineteenth century, when the Company was well established as a dominant political force in India, they serve to demonstrate the complex and multifaceted networks of power, patronage and control that defined the British relationship with India and Indian rulers throughout the period.

Although the Company's power across India generally increased as the eighteenth century wore on, its representatives in Britain were not always pleased by these developments. In fact, as time went on, the Company's very existence as an independent trading body was threatened by its expanding interests and additional responsibilities. One of the main sources of difficulty was the huge amounts of military expenditure required to protect its territories. Lower tax yields than expected compounded the problem. Instead of being an asset, Indian territories were proving to be a liability. Eventually, the government in London was forced to act. First, it intervened and bailed the Company out of its financial crisis. But the problems did not end there. As much as one-third of the population of Bengal was thought to have perished in the famine of 1769–70, a disaster to which the policies of the Company indirectly contributed. Matters had not improved by 1795, when an account pointed out the deplorable state

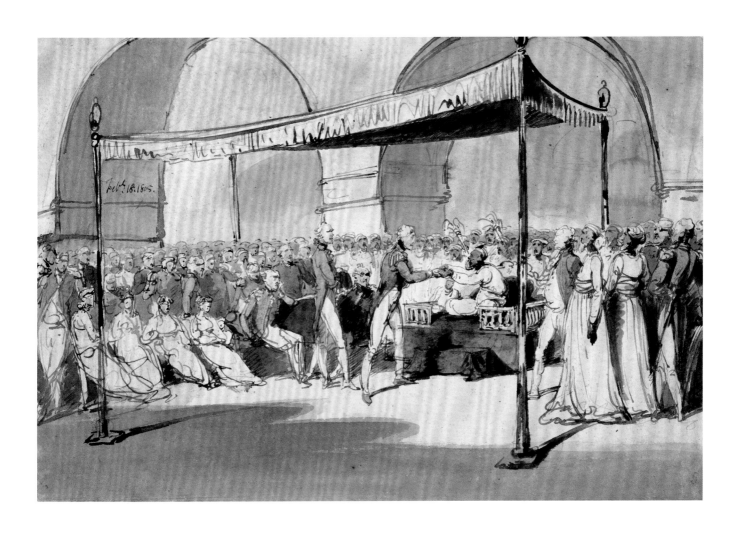

Figure 2.6
George Chinnery,
A Durbar at Madras, 1805 (WD4463)

in which most of the population lived. They 'crowded in narrow huts, which are neither secured from intrusion nor from the weather'; they ate 'unnutritive grains and pulses'; and they wore 'sackcloth and blanket'. The average earnings of a family could 'barely maintain them in the lowest form of subsistence'.[6] All of this meant that the British government came under increased pressure to make the Company more accountable.

A series of bills were introduced in Parliament to curtail the activities of the Company and to bring it much more squarely under government regulation. William Pitt's India Act of 1784 streamlined Company authority in India and established a ministerial Board of Control in London, with responsibility for overseeing Indian affairs. In a separate development, and in one of the most high-profile trials of the age, Warren Hastings was impeached in Parliament on charges of injustice and mis-government. The parliamentary trial of the Company's most senior official in India effectively put the Company and its management of its Indian affairs under sustained public and legal scrutiny. In 1786 Lord Cornwallis was sent to Calcutta as Governor-General with a brief to clean up the Company's operations in India. He reorganised the administration, laying the foundations of the Indian Civil Service, and 'settled' the chaotic revenues of Bengal on a permanent footing. The changes instituted by Cornwallis established administrative and political structures that would remain in place as the East India Company's Raj morphed into the British Raj in the middle of the nineteenth century.

THE COMPANY'S EMPIRE

With the East India Company much more securely under the oversight of the government in London, the final stage of the British rise to dominance in India took place during the wars with Revolutionary and Napoleonic France at the end of the eighteenth and beginning of the nineteenth centuries. A new wave of conquest in the subcontinent was justified by appeals to the distinct possibility of a French assault on India and British trading interests there. Once again, some of the factors for these developments are to be found in the region itself. One of the most important of these was the fact that the Company faced powerful Indian enemies – the Marathas and the Sultans of Mysore – who were rapidly developing sophisticated military power themselves.

To the British, the Marathas were a dangerous group, dedicated to freebooting and plunder. They controlled huge swathes of territory, stretching across central India, and were only finally defeated in the wars of 1817–18. But if the Marathas were regarded with trepidation and fear, the British regarded the rulers of Mysore, in southern India, as an even greater threat. Hyder Ali, Sultan of Mysore from 1761 until 1782, had served as a cavalry subaltern in the armies of the Nizam of Hyderabad (Fig. 2.7). But he rose through the ranks of the army and eventually overthrew the Hindu Wodiyar dynasty, the ruling house of Mysore. As early as 1770, Hyder's Mysore dominated much of the southern uplands of the subcontinent. It was from here that he mounted two successful campaigns, first in 1769 and again in the early 1780s, against the Company's authorities based in Madras. Hyder Ali's victories only seemed to increase his fascination for the British reading and viewing public. In June 1793, for example, the *European*

Figure 2.7
'Hyder Ally Cawn Sitting in his Durbar',
c. 1793 (P368)

Magazine and London Review published an account of 'the tyrant of the East, who raised himself by his abilities to a situation in which by his cruelties he equalled the crimes of Nero or Caligula'. In case any of its readers should forget the threat posed by Hyder, the periodical reminded them that he was 'the scourge of Great Britain and the most formidable enemy (scarcely excepting his son) which the English nation ever experienced in that quarter of the world'.[7]

Hyder Ali's son and successor, Tipu Sultan, continued to preside over 'the most perfect despotism in the world'.[8] But under Richard Wellesley, Lord Mornington (later Marquess Wellesley), who served as Governor-General from 1798 to 1805, Tipu was finally defeated and his capital at Seringapatam seized in 1799. This brought yet another region of India under direct Company control. In July 1800 Wellesley wrote to the Court of Directors in London boasting that 'the glorious termination of the late war in Mysore … established the ascendancy of the British power over all the states of India'. From now on, it would be essential 'to consider the extensive and valuable possessions to the government of which the Company have succeeded, as a great Empire'.[9]

The tussle with Hyder Ali and Tipu, which resulted in four Anglo-Mysore wars, inspired widespread interest among artists and the viewing public. The victory achieved against Tipu on 6 February 1792 was commemorated the following year by an extravagant celebration at the Calcutta Theatre. Among the decorations was one created by

Arthur William Devis and Balthazar Solvyns and partially based on Robert Colebrooke's images:

> In front of the eastern door of the house was a grand transparent view of Seringapatam, by Messrs Devis and Solwyns, from a drawing of Lieutenant Colebrooke. Over the windows were light transparent views of the principal forts taken from the enemy … painted by Mr Solwyns, from drawings of Lieutenant Colebrooke.[10]

Colebrooke, who had served in the Mysore Wars of the early 1780s, published *Twelve Views of Places in the Kingdom of Mysore* in 1794. Alexander Allan published *Views in the Mysore Country* in the same year. The final victory over Tipu, together with the fall of his capital at Seringapatam in 1799, was the occasion for much celebration and led to the creation and dissemination of a plethora of associated images. Established artists in London, Madras and Calcutta announced plans or actually began to work on paintings and projected engravings. At least eight painters – Robert Home, Henry Singleton, Mather Brown, Arthur William Devis, George Carter, James Northcote, Robert Ker Porter and Thomas Stothard – started work on large-scale oil paintings of the event. In 1800 William Sydenham reported from Madras that 'Mr [Thomas] Hickey is to produce seven paintings of the most interesting subjects connected with the late British success in Mysore'.[11]

Perhaps the most ambitious and influential of the visual responses took place in London. There, Robert Ker Porter's panorama of the scene was executed in just six weeks. Porter had spent his youth in Edinburgh, where he determined to become a painter of military subjects. He entered the Royal Academy Schools in February 1791, aged thirteen, having impressed Benjamin West with the vigour and spirit of his sketches. Porter made rapid progress, and he was working as a scene painter for a production of *Othello* at the Lyceum Theatre in London when the *Storming of Seringapatam* appeared. This impressive panorama was 120 feet in length and contained some 700 life-size figures, including portraits of twenty British officers who had played key roles in the battle. Simply displaying the huge picture was a remarkable feat of engineering: it covered 2,550 square feet of canvas and was supported on rollers. Porter's dramatic rendering of the scene placed the victorious British general, David Baird, at the centre and depicted the moment when Tipu's fort was breached simultaneously in two places along its upper walls. The speed with which the entire image, or rather series of images, was executed was clearly meant to capitalise on the interest in and curiosity about the event in Britain. Surviving account books suggest that it was also an extremely lucrative endeavour. It was exhibited at the Lyceum Theatre on 26 April 1800 where crowds lined up to pay the shilling entrance fee. After several months on the Strand, it was sent off to the provinces and Ireland where it drew equally eager crowds. Although the panorama was later destroyed by fire, the surviving original sketches and later engravings made by Giovanni Vendramini help to explain the public fascination with it (Fig. 2.8).

Figure 2.8
Giovanni Vendramini, after Sir Robert Ker Porter,
'The Last Effort of Tippoo Sultaun in Defence of
the Fortress of Seringapatam', 1802 (P778)

Figure 2.9
Henry Tresham,
*Indian Textile Works and Weavers from
the Malabar Coast, c.* 1780 (WD4038)

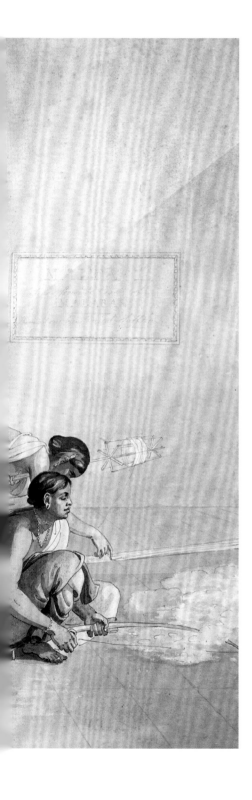

In images as diverse as Benjamin West's painting of the granting of the *diwani* and Robert Ker Porter's panorama of the storming of Seringapatam, we see how artists and visual images played a key role in representing the great events that defined the Company's rise to power. However, it is important not to lose sight of the images that record more commonplace incidents. These also play a role in representing the eighteenth-century India in which the Company exerted increasing control. Henry Tresham's watercolour image of weavers, for example, reminds us that the Company's trading power and commercial wealth were initially based on the lucrative textile trade (Fig. 2.9). The weavers depicted here were probably Tamils, who had migrated to Bengal to escape war and upheaval in other areas of the subcontinent. Tresham was an Irish artist who travelled extensively in Italy but does not seem to have gone to India. Nevertheless, he exhibited this work at the Royal Academy in 1780, indicating the variety of subject matter pertaining to India that found its way to public display.

Artists who had visited and travelled in India were in an even better position to record such scenes. Gavin Hamilton informed his friend Ozias Humphry that Arthur William Devis was travelling upcountry and planning a series on 'the manufactures of India'.[12] Indeed, during his own time in India, Humphry had wanted 'to make sketches of the dresses and manners of the people to work on' when he returned to England.[13] William Hodges also had extensive access to daily life in India. And, although he was celebrated for his thoughtful views of Indian landscape scenes, he also recorded more prosaic activities. His grey-wash image of a budgerow, for instance, silhouettes an Indian craft against a plain background (Fig. 2.10). It might have been sketched quickly as an aide-memoire, or as a study for part of a larger and more complicated painting. Even in this form, however, it underlines the coastal and riverine activities that transported goods and people around India, against the backdrop of which the maritime trade of the East India Company operated.

Of course, it is important to remember that the representation of India and the Company's presence there in many European-produced images masks a wider story of dispossession and violence. The work of artists, as may be imagined, rarely addressed these themes. However, the Company's power was not just evident in its profits, its buildings or its artistic patronage. As we have seen, military power and the implicit threat of violence were key components of its control. The Company had an army in each of its three presidencies (Calcutta, Madras and Bombay), and it relied on thousands of European soldiers and officers, and tens of thousands of Indian sepoys, to maintain its position. By 1761, in the course of the Seven Years War, the Company had some 23,000 sepoys under arms. And this number expanded dramatically so that, by the beginning of the nineteenth century, there were approximately 155,000 sepoys in the Company's service. Three images offer partial insights into this aspect of the Company's activities. The interior view of the Arsenal in Fort William, the Company's fortified stronghold around which grew the city of Calcutta, was produced by William Prinsep (Fig. 2.11). Prinsep was a member of a long-established, well-connected East India Company family. His view provides a graphic reminder of the military and technological power possessed by the Company. And it is further evidence of the underlying

Figure 2.10
William Hodges,
An Indian Sailing Vessel, c. 1780
(YCBA, B1978.43.1751)

The interior of the ARSENAL Fort William

Figure 2.12
Robert Mabon,
Indian Guard Room, late 18th century
(YCBA, B1977.14.22280)

Figure 2.13
Robert Mabon,
A Sepoy Punishment, late 18th century
(YCBA, B1977.14.22284)

threat of violence that ran in parallel with its economic and political control. Robert Mabon served in the Company's army, and his views of life in the military are clearly based on personal experience. In a sketch of the *Indian Guard Room*, or the *Punch Tent in Camp*, Mabon offers a charming image that conveys the soldiers relaxing (Fig. 2.12). Reliance on alcohol was a key part of their recreational activity and the image is inscribed with a telling motto: 'For arrack inspires us and fires us with courage, love and joy &tc.' In sharp contrast, his image of a sepoy being flogged is rather less light-hearted and serves to underline the interplay between political power, military control and the threat of violence that helped to sustain the Company's position in the subcontinent (Fig. 2.13).

WAY STATIONS

Although the East India Company's rise to power was a complicated one, and followed a tortuous path of political intrigue and military might, it had its origins in trade. At its simplest, the Company was precisely that: a commercial company whose objective was to increase trade and maximise profit for its shareholders. Its success depended on mobility. The ability to travel back and forth between Britain and India required skill and leadership, as well as sturdy vessels and convenient ports. Maritime connections and communications were the foundations on which all of the Company's activities were built. As a result, the Company was keen to ensure easy access to refuelling and refreshment points along the sea route to Asia. Therefore, although they were far removed from the Indian subcontinent, islands like St Helena and places like the Cape of Good Hope played a key strategic and practical role for the Company and its shipping. In India itself, the great coastal cities of Madras, Bombay and Calcutta grew out of the Company's shipping and commercial activities. It is perhaps unsurprising, then, that the Company's London headquarters was filled with pictures of such ports, while prints of these places found ready markets elsewhere.

East India Company vessels, such as the *Earl of Abergavenny*, depicted by Thomas Luny, were usually rounder in shape than ships of the Royal Navy as they were designed to carry large quantities of cargo rather than for speed and manoeuvrability in battle (Fig. 2.14). The hold at the bottom of the ship and the lower of the two decks were used mostly for cargo and storage, while the upper deck was reserved as living quarters for the men. They ate and slept in these cramped surroundings, between the cannon which were used for defence and ceremonial salutes. The journey to India could take up to eight months, and involved crossing the equator twice and sailing through the watery expanses of both the Atlantic and the Indian oceans. But crossing the ocean was not necessarily as featureless as it sounds: there were landscapes to experience and sights to record. Ozias Humphry, for example, who travelled to India in 1785, assiduously recorded in his sketchbook the scenes and places he encountered on the route to Asia (Fig. 2.15).

Humphry's images remind us that certain places along the route had particular significance for East India Company ships and their passengers. On long sea journeys to Asia, the principal value of these locations was as revictualling points, where fresh

Figure 2.14
Thomas Luny,
*The 'Earl of Abergavenny', East Indiaman,
off Southsea*, 1801 (F59)

Figure 2.15
Ozias Humphry,
*From Col. Martin's guest room,
Jan. 16, 1786, Lucknow*, 1786
(Add. MS 15959, f. 2r)

Figure 2.16
George Lambert and Samuel Scott,
The Island of St Helena, c. 1731 (F37)

supplies of water, fruit, vegetables and meat could be taken on. They also offered strategic advantages for the Company, providing safe and secure havens for its ships on their passage to and, most importantly, from India when they were laden with valuable cargo. Ships could call at a bewildering variety of places: Madeira, the Canary Islands, and the Cape Verde Islands off the coast of North Africa; Rio de Janeiro, St Helena and Cape Town in the South Atlantic; and various places in the Seychelles and the Comoros Islands in the Indian Ocean.

The importance of such locations on the passage to India can be seen in a series of paintings commissioned by the Company to adorn the Directors' Court Room in Leadenhall Street. The Company minutes for November 1732 record that a total of six pictures were commissioned from George Lambert and Samuel Scott, at a cost of fifteen guineas each. The commission reflects the Company's willingness to use art in order to convey an image of power to itself and others. That two of the six paintings represent St Helena and Cape Town also underlines the importance of these particular way stations for the Company's commercial endeavours. Lambert was primarily an architectural, landscape and scene painter, while Scott specialised in ships and marine painting. Between the two of them, they offered a series of composite scenes that profiled the Company's shipping power against a variety of shore establishments stretching across the breadth of its maritime world. Since the artists did not travel to India, they probably worked from early eighteenth-century plans of the various settlements, although liberties were certainly taken over the architectural details and some of their sources were topographically obsolete. The image of Cape Town, for instance, seems to have been based on a seventeenth-century painting of Table Bay, with the dominant image of Table Mountain in the background, the walled fortifications and warehouses on the shore and Dutch ships in the bay. Nevertheless, in terms of subject matter, the images convey the bustling trade and maritime activity across a huge expanse of ocean that helped to elevate the Company to its position of power. As a whole, the group of half a dozen pictures reminded the directors of the global geography of the Company's activities and emphasised the dependence of shipping and maritime trade on shore-based factories and ports.

Despite its remote location in the tempestuous waters of the South Atlantic – the nearest continental landfall is over 1,200 miles away in southern Africa – St Helena was part of Britain's Asian empire since the earliest days of the East India Company's trading ventures (Fig. 2.16). English interest was represented in the seventeenth century in the form of a charter to govern the island granted by Oliver Cromwell in 1657 and the decision by the East India Company to fortify and colonise it the following year. The Company's interest in the island was confirmed at the Restoration in 1660 when it received a royal charter and, by the 1680s, it was regularly referred to as 'The Company's Island'.[14] In 1792 Robert Brooke, St Helena's governor, composed an account of his bailiwick which emphasised the advantages that it brought to the Company's endeavours. Helpfully, the island offered secure anchorage: along the whole leeward coast 'ships may anchor under 23 fathom water in perfect security in all seasons of the year'. Brooke went on:

Figure 2.17
George Lambert and Samuel Scott,
The Cape of Good Hope, *c.* 1731 (F35)

> The island has been esteemed valuable merely on account of its situation, being safe and commodious at all seasons for ships to touch at returning from India, that its waters are excellent, and that those afflicted with the scurvy recover more rapidly on its shores than on any other perhaps in the world.[15]

The fruitful possibilities of the island were just one of the reasons cited for retaining it, however. Jacob Bosanquet, a Company director, regarded it as 'the principal link of that chain which connects this country with her Indian possessions and of undoubted great importance'.[16]

The Cape of Good Hope, at the southern tip of Africa, was similarly prized. Located at an important strategic site, halfway between Asia and Europe, the area around Cape Town was first settled by the Dutch East India Company in 1652, when they established a base there to provide their vessels with fresh provisions and water. By the eighteenth century, ships of all nations and companies were taking advantage of its harbour and onshore facilities. Indeed, by the middle of the century, about half of the ships in port at any one time belonged to the British East India Company. The strategic position and other benefits offered by this convenient location, captured in Lambert and Scott's image, continued to grow in importance throughout the period (Fig. 2.17). Eventually, the danger of allowing it to fall into the hands of their principal continental rival forced the hand of the British government, and they sent an expeditionary force to seize the colony in 1795 during the war with Revolutionary France. Although it was returned briefly to the Batavian (Dutch) Republic in 1803, following the Treaty of Amiens, the Cape was taken once again at the end of 1805 and it remained British throughout the course of the nineteenth century.

While these two locations were among the most important for the refuelling and revictualling of Company ships on their voyages to and from Asia, it was in their views of the great Indian coastal cities that Lambert and Scott represented the beating heart of the Company's operations. Madras, Bombay and Calcutta represented the key sites for the Company in India. They made the Company's political power and economic success possible.

PORT CITIES

Although the Company traded from Surat, on the north-west coast, in its early days, the first permanent Company fortress in India was at Fort St George. The areas around Madras (present-day Chennai) initially attracted the Portuguese and the Dutch, both of whom had settled in the region before the arrival of the English East India Company in the early seventeenth century. A survey of the Coromandel, or south-eastern, coast of the subcontinent by Francis Day brought a fishing village called Madraspatnam to his attention. In 1639 Day managed to secure from the local governor the right to build a fort and castle on a strip of land about three miles in length. It was not until the following year that the first English settlement was officially established when the fortified enclosure was completed on St George's Day, 23 April 1640, and named Fort St George (Figs 2.18 and 2.19). This was the East India Company's principal

Figure 2.18
George Lambert and Samuel Scott,
Fort St George, Madras, c. 1731 (F46)

settlement in India until 1774, when Calcutta was officially declared to be the seat of government.

Most European depictions of the city in the early eighteenth century, such as those by Lambert and Scott and by Jan Van Ryne, focus on the solid mass of the Company's fortified warehouses and the shipping traffic they facilitated. But around this centre of activity a new metropolis was growing. The city of Madras developed through the gradual assimilation of Fort St George into the mass of the so-called 'Blacktown' inhabited by Tamil- and Telugu-speaking merchants, Armenians and Indo-Portuguese. After 1763, the Brahmin town of Triplicane and the palaces of the Nawab of Arcot were also gradually incorporated as suburbs. Until the turn of the nineteenth century, Madras flourished as an exporter of fine cloth. Thereafter, it lost some of its commercial pre-eminence to Bombay. But it retained its status as an important centre of government, and this was expressed in the imposing colonial architecture that was often recorded in prints and drawings of the city around this time. Fort St George was enlarged, for example, and a Government House was built inside its fortifications. In their engraving, Thomas and William Daniell depicted the colonnaded veranda of Government House rising above the fort wall (Fig. 2.20). The tower of St Mary's Church, before the spire was added, can be seen to the right of the flag. The rather two-dimensional view of the city, seen from the waterfront, in earlier images has been replaced here with a more dynamic composition which serves to bring the viewer into the heart of the city, adding depth and perspective to the scene. In the letterpress to accompany the engraving, the Daniells described the fort as being 'considered by engineers as a work of very great strength'. But they also commented on the changing nature of land usage which would continue to characterise developments in the nineteenth century as British administrators sought to escape the unforgiving climate:

> The business of the English at Madras is chiefly transacted within the fort; but in general the opulent have houses in the country a few miles from it, as the heat of the air within the fort, owing to the quantity of the masonry and closeness of the buildings is found very oppressive.[17]

In their 'South East View of Fort St George, Madras', the Daniells combined an interest in the East India Company's presence, represented by the buildings of the fort and the architecture of the city, with the impressive natural setting around which the fortress had initially developed (Fig. 2.21):

> This view is taken on the beach southward of the Fort of Madras; the larger building to the right of the flag-staff is the new exchange, and the higher one to the left is the church, to which a spire has been added since the taking of this view in the year 1793.[18]

Some years after the Daniells' visit, John Gantz's watercolour drawing of Bentinck's Buildings and the beach illustrates the city's continued importance (Fig. 2.23). Gantz

Figure 2.19
After Jan Van Ryne,
'Fort of St George on the Coromandel Coast, Madras,
Belonging to the East India Company of England', *c.* 1754
(P236)

Figure 2.20
Thomas Daniell and William Daniell,
'The Government House, Fort St George, Madras',
Oriental Scenery, II, plate 9, 1816 (10.Tab.30(2))

Figure 2.21
Thomas Daniell and William Daniell,
'Western Entrance of Fort St George',
Oriental Scenery, II, plate 12, 1816 (10.Tab.30(2))

Figure 2.22
Thomas Daniell and William Daniell,
'South East View of Fort St George, Madras',
Oriental Scenery, II, plate 7, 1816 (10.Tab.30(2))

was employed as a draftsman and surveyor by the East India Company, while Bentinck's Buildings were erected as mercantile offices during the administration of Lord William Bentinck, who served as governor between 1803 and 1807.

However, notwithstanding its imposing architecture and its importance as a commercial and administrative centre, one of the features of Madras most commonly remarked upon by eighteenth-century European visitors was the view of the city from the sea. The approach to the city was one of the defining moments of British travellers' encounters with India, and looms large in both texts and images of the city. William Hodges offered his thoughts upon first encountering Madras from the water in typically artistic and aesthetic terms:

> The English town, rising from within Fort St George, has from the sea a rich and beautiful appearance; the houses being covered with a stucco called chunam, which in itself is nearly as compact as the finest marble, and, as it bears as high a polish, is equally splendid with that elegant material. The stile of the buildings is in general handsome. They consist of long colonnades, with open porticoes, and flat roofs, and offer to the eye an appearance similar to what we may conceive of a Grecian city in the age of Alexander.[19]

In 1792 James Main, a gardener who had travelled to India in order to collect rare and valuable plants, presented a textual picture of the scene that would find visual equivalence in the work of a number of artists:

> Madras has no harbour, but has an open roadstead on an extended level shore, covered chiefly with groves of cocoa-nut trees. Landing through a heavy surf is not a pleasing matter to a timid stranger; for though there is no serious fear of loss of life, there is every chance of a good ducking. The skill and amphibious character of the poor naked creatures, who guide the large tub-like boats on the tops and in the shallow valleys between the impetuous waves, is our security; and they seldom fail in taking advantage of a careering wave to land high and dry upon the beach.[20]

Even in their 'South East View of Fort St George, Madras' (Fig. 2.22), the Daniells felt compelled to comment on Madras's maritime aspect:

> In the distance is seen part of the Madras roads; and in the foreground the sea breaking in with its usual turbulency on this coast; the only vessels in use for passing through this surge to communicate with the shipping, are called Massoola boats. They are flat bottomed and built without iron, the planks being sewed together with line made from the outer coat of the cocoa nut.[21]

Unlike northern India, Madras receives a double monsoon: from the east between July and September and from the west between October and December. Fort St George

Figure 2.23
John Gantz,
*North East View of Bentinck's
Buildings, Madras*, 1822
(WD1362)

was completely unprotected from the sea until the construction of a harbour in the late nineteenth century. Before then, ships had to anchor in the roads and land their passengers and cargoes by means of small boats. Simple wooden boats, *masula*, were used to transport people and goods through the heavy surf and then boatsmen would carry the passengers ashore on their shoulders (Fig. 2.24).

Madras's importance on the east coast was matched by Bombay's on the west, which grew to become a great centre of British commerce by the early nineteenth century. Its harbour was 'reputed one of the most famous Havens of all the Indies, as never being choked up by the Storms, or yearly Monsoons, but affords at all Seasons, Reception and Security for whole Fleets'.[22] Initially it was Surat, to the north, that acted as the official commercial headquarters of the East India Company in western India. As early as 1652, however, the Company turned its attention to a small Portuguese settlement further south which it considered purchasing in order to avoid constant conflict with the Mughal governor of Surat. In 1661 Alphonso VI of Portugal presented Bombay to Charles II as part of the dowry of his sister, Catherine of Braganza. In 1668 it was leased by the Crown to the Company for £10 per annum and Sir George Oxenden, President of Surat, became its first governor. At the outset, the city's fortunes were chequered. In its

Figure 2.24
George Chinnery,
Surf Boats on the Beach, Madras, 1807
(WD147)

Figure 2.25
George Lambert and Samuel Scott,
Bombay, c. 1731 (F48)

Figure 2.26
James Wales,
'View of Bombay Harbour', *Bombay Views:
Twelve Views of the Island of Bombay and
its Vicinity Taken in the Years 1791 and 1792*,
plate 1, 1800 (Maps 7 TAB.20.no.1)

early years, Bombay was a small and frequently embattled station, which the Company considered relinquishing on a number of occasions. In the 1680s, for example, it was occupied for nearly a year by English mutineers and 'pirates'. And the Marathas were a constant, if diminishing, threat throughout the eighteenth century. But its fine deep-water harbour and the access it offered to the Arabian Sea, western Indian Ocean and coastal trade routes soon helped to build up a cosmopolitan trading community, which attracted Portuguese settlers from Goa, Muslim merchants from Arabia, rich Gujarati Hindu traders and, after the 1740s, Parsis from Surat who worked as shipwrights and helped to build up the powerful Bombay mercantile fleet. By the 1780s, when the Maratha threat had been largely contained and the city had begun to act as an entrepôt in the opium and raw cotton trades to China, Bombay's rise to prosperity was assured.

The view of Bombay by George Lambert and Samuel Scott gives a snapshot of its development in the first sixty years under Company control (Fig. 2.25). The large white building in the centre, with the gateway surmounted by a coat of arms, is probably the warehouse marked in Grose's map of 1750. On the right, a Union flag can be seen flying above the castle while a large vessel in the foreground wears the Company's distinctive red and white colours. As with the other views painted for the Directors' Court Room, this image focuses squarely on the fort and the shipping, the twin concerns of the East India Company at this time. Bombay had developed considerably when James Wales's views of the city were published in 1800. In the first two images in the series – depicting the harbour – large and small boats, both Indian and European, ply their trade in the natural harbour created by the seven islands that constituted the city (Figs. 2.26 and 2.27). Here is a busy and bustling working dock with Indian figures and bales of cargo, ocean-going ships and the mountains of the Western Ghats in the distance. In

Figure 2.27
James Wales,
'View of Bombay Harbour', *Bombay Views: Twelve Views of the
Island of Bombay and its Vicinity Taken in the Years 1791 and 1792*,
plate 2, 1800 (Maps 7 TAB.20.no.2)

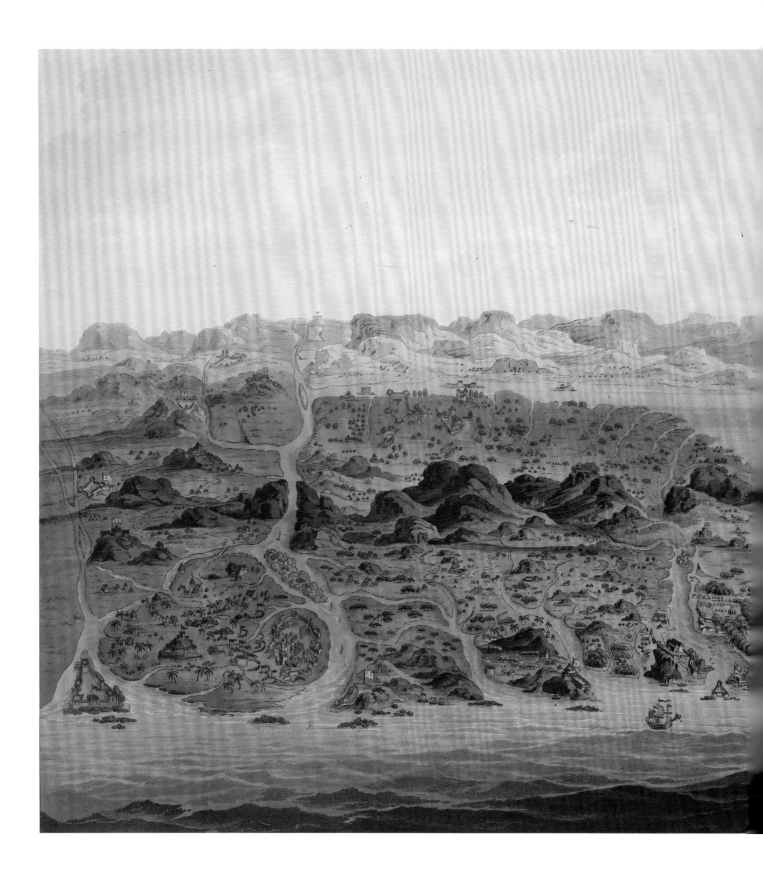

Figure 2.28
J. S. Barth,
'Islands of Bombay and Salsette', 1803
(Maps K.Top. 115.58.d.2)

these coastal scenes, Wales presents viewers with a geographical and metaphorical portal to the interior of the subcontinent.

Calcutta was the capital of British India and the focus for much of the commercial, political and artistic activity that defined the British presence in the subcontinent. It was a magnet for Company officials and, as we have seen, many of the artists attempting to forge new careers for themselves made directly for the city. It was, as a result, one of the most frequently represented places in India. Artists offered a variety of perspectives (literally and metaphorically) on its river, its scenery, its waterfront, its buildings and its people.

Though it was eventually to become the 'second city' of the British Empire, Calcutta had an inauspicious start. It was established in marshy swamp lands near Hooghly by Job Charnock in 1690. Until the early years of the eighteenth century, Madras and Surat were much more important to the Company's trade. But the extraordinary productivity of Bengal's weavers and the opportunities for lucrative inland or 'country' trade up the rivers Ganges and Jumna soon began to work in Calcutta's favour. By the middle of the century, Calcutta was a rich commercial city. It was the centre for the huge trade conducted by the East India Company in what had become, as we have seen, a virtually autonomous province. From both the city itself and a series of subordinate commercial 'factories' in other parts of Bengal, the Company procured its cargoes for London, consisting largely of cotton cloth and silk. An engraving by Jan Van Ryne shows shipping on the Hooghly River and the old Fort William which was soon to

Figure 2.29
After Jan Van Ryne,
'Fort William in the Kingdom of Bengal',
1754 (P462)

Figure 2.30
Thomas Daniell and William Daniell,
'The Old Fort, the Playhouse,
Holwell's Monument', *Views of
Calcutta*, plate 1, 1786 (P88)

Figure 2.31
Francis Jukes,
'View of a House, Manufactory and
Bazaar in Calcutta', 1795 (P2382)

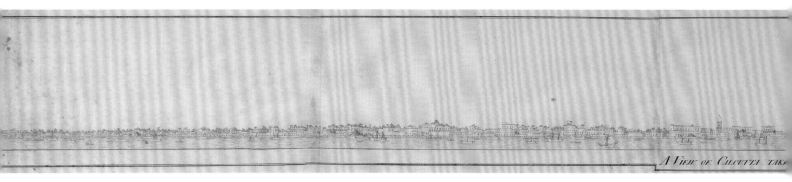

A View of Calcutta taken

fall victim to attack by the Nawab, Siraj-ud-Daulah, in 1756 (Fig. 2.29). Van Ryne, who settled in London around 1750, had never visited India. Like the views by Lambert and Scott, Van Ryne's image is almost topographical in its horizontal format and focus. The fort, the landing stage with a crane and the factory building are clearly visible, while the Governor's private residence, with its avenue of trees leading down to the river, is also represented. St Anne's Church, to the left of Government House, is shown with a wooden bell-cote (the spire had fallen during a cyclone in 1757).

The boom in trade after the Battle of Plassey swelled the population of Calcutta to well over 100,000. A large Company garrison was placed at a newly constructed Fort William and, in the 1770s, the city became the seat of the Governor-General and the headquarters of the major army and naval commands. William Hodges remarked on this turnaround in the city's fortunes: 'Calcutta, from a small and inconsiderable fort … and a few warehouses, was soon raised to a great and opulent city, when the government of the kingdom of Bengal fell into the hands of the English.'[23] Something of this increased importance is captured in the Daniells' view of 'The Old Fort, the Playhouse, Holwell's Monument' in their *Views of Calcutta* (Fig. 2.30). This image seems to encapsulate power. The eastern wall of Old Fort William is on the left, while on the right is the memorial to the tragedy of the Black Hole. The theatre in the centre ground was built by public subscription in 1775 while, on the extreme right, we can see part of the Writers' Building built in 1780 by Company engineer Thomas Lyon. Although it was the centre of East India Company power, Calcutta was also an Indian city. Merchants and local agents built townhouses for themselves and embellished the city with temples, all of which rivalled the great examples of Company architecture (Fig. 2.31).

Not everyone was impressed by the city. In 1780, for instance, Calcutta was described as 'that scattered and confused chaos of houses, huts, sheds, streets and lanes, alleys, windings, gutters, sinks and tanks, which jumbled into an undistinguished mass of corruption, equally offensive to human sense and health'.[24] In general, however, the city's imposing natural and man-made features won over those approaching it. The earliest view of the new fort at Calcutta was given in Antoine Polier's *A View of Calcutta Taken from the Other Side of the River in the Year 1768* (Fig. 2.32). Polier was an engineer rather than a professional artist. He became Chief Engineer of the Bengal Army in 1762 and, six years later, in 1768, he was in Calcutta commanding the garrison and working on the new fort.

As with other Indian cities, new arrivals to Calcutta were much struck by the approach from the water and the initial appearance of the fort, which seemed to

Figure 2.32
Antoine Polier,
A View of Calcutta Taken from the Other Side of the River in the Year 1768, 1768 (WD4148)

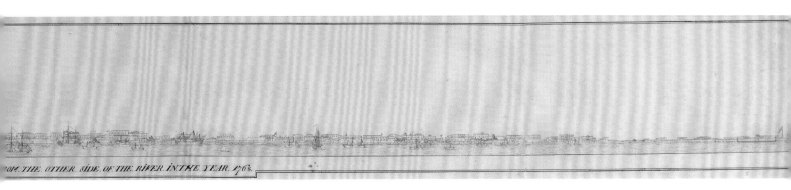

ON THE OTHER SIDE OF THE RIVER IN THE YEAR 1788.

dominate the scene as boats came upriver from Garden Reach. John Prinsep, arriving in 1771, remarked on how 'the stream seemed to widen as we proceeded and straight before us we beheld a stately forest of masts, vessels, an immense city and the bustle of commercial business'. He made comparisons with a European equivalent: 'Next, the fort opened to our view reminding me of Valenciennes, regular, majestic and commanding.'[25] Mrs Eliza Fay was similarly impressed nine years later:

> The banks of the river are as one may say absolutely studded with elegant mansions. … These houses are surrounded by groves and lawns, which descend to the water's edge, and present a constant succession of whatever can delight the eye, or bespeak wealth and eloquence in the owners. The noble appearance of the river also, which is much wider than the Thames at London Bridge, together with the amazing variety of vessels continually passing on its surface, add to the beauty of the scene.

And she went on:

> The town of Calcutta reaches along the eastern bank of the Hoogly; as you come up past Fort William and the Esplanada it has a beautiful appearance. Esplanade-row, as it is called, which fronts the Fort, seems to be composed of palaces: the whole range, except what is taken up by the Government and Council Houses, is occupied by the principal gentlemen in the settlement – no person being allowed to reside in Fort William, but such as are attached to the army, gives it greatly the advantage over Fort St George.

To her eyes the fort was 'so well kept and every thing in such excellent order, that it is quite a curiosity to see it – all the slopes, banks, and ramparts, are covered with the richest verdure, which completes the enchantment of the scene'.[26] A French visitor in 1790, Louis de Grandpré, described it as 'not only the handsomest town in Asia but one of the finest in the world'.[27] William Hodges was another who was suitably moved: 'A European lands here in the midst of a great city.' Sailing up the Hooghly River in March 1781, he was struck with the beauty of the scene:

> The vessel had no sooner gained one other reach of the river than the whole city of Calcutta bursts upon the eye. This capital of the British dominions in the East

Figure 2.33
William Byrne, after William Hodges,
'A View of Calcutta taken from Fort William',
in William Hodges, *Travels in India, during the Years
1780, 1781, 1782 & 1783*, plate 2, 1793 (W2126(2))

Figure 2.34
William Hodges,
View of Calcutta from Garden Reach House, c. 1781
(YCBA, B1978.43.1779)

Figure 2.35
Samuel Davis,
Calcutta, late 18th century
(YCBA, B1986.29.586)

is marked by a considerable fortress ... superior to any in India. On the foreground of the picture is the water-gate of the fort, which reflects great honour on the talents of the engineer – the ingenious Colonel Polier. The glacis and esplanade are seen in perspective, bounded by a range of beautiful and regular buildings; and a considerable reach of the river, with vessels of various classes and sizes, from the largest Indiamen to the smallest boats of the country, closes the scene.[28]

Hodges not only described Calcutta effusively – he painted it at least five times (Figs. 2.33 and 2.34).

The East India Company, which provided the circumstances to nurture so much artistic talent, depended on its servants' ability to respond to the constantly changing political climate in India. Securing power and protecting trade were equally reliant on access to port facilities and maritime communications. These aspects of the Company's story feature in all kinds of artistic records. But, for the vast majority of those who travelled to its shores with the aim of picturing India, their real joy was in the people and places they encountered there.

CHAPTER 3
Places

The landscapes of India provided some of the richest and most enduring aspects of the British engagement with the subcontinent in the eighteenth and nineteenth centuries. Indian cities and countryside presented a wealth of 'valuable subjects for the painter'.[1] India's great rivers, wide plains and imposing mountain ranges provided unrivalled visual raw material. And this natural beauty was complemented by evidence of the human presence in the landscape: imposing architectural monuments, temples, mosques, bridges and even ruins. This chapter charts some of the ways in which artists responded to these subjects. William Hodges offers a useful introduction to the representation of landscape. Not only was he well connected in East India Company circles in Bengal, making him party to the latest thinking of Company officials like Warren Hastings, but he was also a genuine artistic innovator. His time with James Cook, on his voyages of exploration to the South Pacific, as well as his own artistic training, made Hodges acutely aware of the power of landscape. And his work in India goes beyond the topographical recording of places to convey something of the artist's personal response to the sights before him. In considering Hodges's thoughtful engagement with Indian landscape scenes, we are led to one of the central themes in this chapter: the importance of aesthetic and artistic influences on artists. What role did philosophical concepts like the picturesque or the sublime play in creating images of India? Should Indian landscapes reflect or attempt to convey, in some way, the comforts of 'home'? Or should artists seek out and emphasise the unusual and the extraordinary: things that would immediately advertise India's difference from everything European?

But the immensity, grandeur and sheer visual excitement on display in India could not be contained wholly within aesthetic categories. And artistic sensibilities were not immune from the scale and beauty of the landscape or the variety and antiquity of the architecture. The chapter moves on, then, to consider artists who were inspired by the evidence before their eyes. People like James Baillie Fraser, Samuel Davis and the Daniells were inspired to travel across India and to record scenes and locations for European audiences. Their journeys followed the geographical contours determined by the political and imperial reach of the East India Company, and the visual records derived from these travels similarly contain elements of that encounter between East and West.

The chapter concludes by considering the human element that underpinned all of these representations. Whether they were inspired by classical precedents or by everyday activities, artists used scenes of landscape to comment on the human condition, as they saw it, in India. Landscape offered a visual directory of human activity over the centuries: the influence of religion, the movement of people, the rise and fall of empires, the advance of technology. And certain places were especially important focal points: the Taj Mahal at Agra and the Hindu holy city of Benares, for example, offered particularly impressive visual material for European artists. In representing these places in their own distinctive style, these artists played their part in creating visual expectations in viewers that would endure for centuries.

Figure 3.1
William Hodges,
'View of the Rajmahal Hills with a
Sentenial [*sic*] in the Foreground', *c.* 1781
(YCBA, B1978.43.1740)

THE LANDSCAPES OF WILLIAM HODGES: BLAZING A TRAIL

The work of William Hodges offers interesting examples of the central role that landscape played in British visions of India. His skills and experiences as a painter meant that he evinced an unusually varied response to the landscapes of the subcontinent in his work. As a young man, Hodges had learned the classical picturesque formula for landscape from his mentor, Richard Wilson: to compose his paintings carefully, to manipulate and rearrange topography if required for the sake of effect, and even to introduce imaginary details as a means of instilling a sense of calm and order. But, during his time on James Cook's expedition to the South Pacific, Hodges became one of the earliest professional artists to experiment with painting *en plein air* in an attempt to capture the fleeting effects of light, atmosphere and climate that he witnessed all around him. These experiences gave Hodges an unrivalled knowledge of different ways of composing landscape, and honed his judgement about the best way to present a scene for maximum visual impact. He put these lessons into practice during his time in India. As well as being patronised by Warren Hastings, Hodges made three tours from Calcutta: starting each time along the river Ganges and encountering towns of historical and architectural interest. Visiting Benares on his first tour, he reached as far as Agra on his third and most extensive tour, where he also saw the Taj Mahal. These travels gave Hodges a keen understanding of the possibilities for landscape artists working in India and he recorded his

Figure 3.2
William Hodges,
*Storm on the Ganges, with Mrs Hastings
near the Col-gon Rocks*, 1790
(YCBA, B1973.1.23)

ideas in both images and text, giving us a valuable insight into his thoughts about the art of landscape (Fig. 3.1).

Hodges strove to understand the complex cultures and religions that he found around him in India. Rather like his work on the second of Cook's Pacific voyages, he provides eloquent visual commentary on the societies through which he passed. Through the variety of his artistic and textual output, then, Hodges brought out the rich and complex history of India evident in its monuments, temples, scholarship and people. In many ways, Hodges thought of his representation of Indian landscape as a contribution to the understanding and interpretation of the ancient cultures of India, a process that was then current among many Europeans in the subcontinent (see Chapter 4). For Hodges, India was just as interesting, if not more so, than the classical civilisations of Greece and Rome to which educated eighteenth-century Europeans turned so frequently. Indeed, in a provocative pronouncement published in *A Dissertation on the Prototypes of Architecture, Hindoo, Moorish and Gothic* (1787), he asserted that Indian monuments, because of their antiquity, were the origin of some of the forms and details for which ancient Greek and Roman architecture were celebrated.

Hodges's impressive rendition of a storm on the river Ganges encapsulates something of his working methods in India, and his use of landscape for both intellectual and visual effect (Fig. 3.2). On one level, the picture records a scene of deep personal interest for Hodges's patron, Warren Hastings, depicting the events of 1782 when Hastings fell gravely ill and his wife made a dangerous voyage of three days down the Ganges to be with him. It subsequently became the focus of Hastings's art collection at Daylesford, his country residence in Gloucestershire, where it hung above the chimney-piece in the picture room there. But it is more than a mere transcription of an event. Instead, it is an attempt by Hodges to use local circumstances, climate and light to convey a broader point about the human condition. The composition and pictorial elements are carefully deployed to create a sense of the landscape functioning as an allegory of the trials and dangers of human existence. Hodges was familiar with this part of the river from his time in India, and he described it in his *Travels in India*:

> The country about Colgong is, I think, the most beautiful I have seen in India. The waving appearance of the land, its fine turf and detached woods, backed by the extensive forests on the hills, brought to my mind many of the fine parks in England; and its overlooking the Ganges, which has more the appearance of an ocean at this place than of a river, gives the prospect inexpressible grandeur.[2]

In this image, however, Hodges used the elements that comprised the landscape to add dynamism and drama. The scene is suffused with energy and the possibility of impending disaster. Mrs Hastings is hidden beneath the white canopy of the small vessel and only the figures of the boatmen are visible. Their fate hangs in the balance as the crew of Indians, grasping at oars and the tiller, engage in a desperate struggle to guide the boat between the forbidding rocks and the fierce water. The vessel navigates a treacherous path between the shore in the darkened foreground of the picture,

Figure 3.3
William Hodges,
View of Warren Hastings's House at Alipur
and Two Figures in the Foreground, c. 1782
(YCBA, B1978.43.1783)

Figure 3.4
William Hodges,
*Marmalong Bridge, with a Sepoy and Natives
in the Foreground*, 1783 (YCBA, B1974.3.8)

where an ominously barren tree reaches out over the rapids, and an island in the river to the right. This island, where a tree in full leaf emerges in the sunlight beyond the storm, together with a bright rainbow springing upwards over the entire scene, seems to promise a brighter future once the trial of the storm has been endured and overcome. The equivalence between the painted scene and the condition of Hastings at this time hardly needs to be underlined. But Hodges's success in creating such a powerful and evocative visual image alludes both to his prowess as an artist and to the power of landscape painting in his hands.

Despite his willingness to experiment with new forms and techniques, Hodges never discounted the more traditional European aesthetic forms of representing landscape when he deemed them suitable for his purposes. In some of his work for Warren Hastings, for example, he introduced the European presence into the Indian landscape using elements drawn from the tenets of the picturesque. His canvas depicting Hastings's house at Alipur offers a visual equivalent to the judgement of Benjamin Mee, a Calcutta-based merchant and financier (Fig. 3.3). Mee wrote to his brother-in-law in Hampshire, offering the opinion that 'Mr Hodges' pictures of India make it look like noblemen's seats'.[3] Although the large tree in the foreground and the two figures serve to anchor the scene firmly in India, the presence of the European residence appears to be a natural feature of the landscape and not unlike many pictures of grand country houses in Britain being painted at the time. Hodges's landscapes also give us an insight into his views about the current state of India. His depiction of the so-called Marmalong Bridge, for instance, provides evidence of the positive influence of outsiders on the landscape of India (Fig. 3.4). The bridge, initially funded by an Armenian merchant, might be seen as an example of these outsiders' capacity to improve India by their presence. The parallel with the East India Company, and Hastings's activities in India on its behalf, could not have been clearer.

THE AESTHETICS OF LANDSCAPE: THE COMFORTS OF HOME

An interest in landscape was not confined to William Hodges, of course. Representations of landscape in eighteenth-century Britain were central to artistic practice and to notions of national and cultural identity. Unsurprisingly then, artistic training and aesthetic ideas acquired in Europe made a significant impact on the way in which artists responded to Indian scenes. The visual representation of India by British artists was heavily influenced by artistic and aesthetic preferences in Europe. Ideas about what made a good picture, what comprised an interesting view or what constituted an aesthetically pleasing composition were deeply affected by prevailing fashions and trends in European art. In some cases, they drew on specific philosophical criteria in order to compose their images and to convey their impressions of India. Ideas of the picturesque, for example, encouraged people to look at nature as they would view a painting. Simply put, the picturesque meant literally 'like a picture'. Landscapes in this mode were harmonious and coherently composed. Irregularity, abrupt shapes and outlines, and intricate details were permitted too, however, as a way of underlining the 'naturalness' of the scene.

One of the results of such depictions was the creation of aesthetic and visual connections with Europe. Thousands of miles away from their familiar surroundings, travellers and artists arriving in India sought visual equivalences with home where they could find them and created them where they could not. Some of the more salubrious areas around Calcutta, where many European servants of the East India Company had their residences, were just such places where these connections with home were found or manufactured. Here the representation of landscape served to collapse the distance between India and Britain.

Garden Reach – a few miles downriver from the centre of Calcutta – was particularly lauded by travellers. It was 'studded with elegant mansions' and surrounded by charming lawns and 'groves', according to Eliza Fay.[4] When he passed by in November 1777, William Hickey was 'greatly pleased by a rich and magnificent view of a number of splendid houses. … The verdure throughout on every side was beautiful beyond imagination, the whole of the landscape being more luxuriant than I had any expectation of seeing in the burning climate of Bengal.'[5] And the remarks of the tea merchant Thomas Twining, upon first seeing the scene, are indicative of how other Europeans viewed it at the time:

> Handsome villas lined the left or southern bank, and on the opposite shore was the residence of the superintendent of the Company's botanical garden. It was a large upper-roomed house not many yards from the river, along the edge of which the garden itself extended. The situation of the elegant garden houses, as the villas on the left bank were called, surrounded by verdant grounds laid out in the English style, with the Ganges flowing before them, covered with boats and shipping, struck me, as it does everybody who sees it for the first time, as singularly delightful. These charming residences announced our approach to the modern capital of the East, and bespoke the wealth and luxury of its inhabitants.[6]

The scene may have announced the approach of Calcutta but it did so in decidedly European terms.

And these textual descriptions found a visual equivalence in Thomas and William Daniell's depiction of Garden Reach, which was published as a print in their *A Picturesque Voyage to India by the Way of China* in 1810 (Fig. 3.5). The scene incorporates a view of Calcutta in the distance, with the imposing Government House silhouetted against the skyline. The inclusion of this structure underlines the importance and power of the East India Company which underpinned the British presence in Bengal and made scenes such as these at Garden Reach possible. Indeed, the history and evolution of the image itself provides a salutary reminder of the momentous changes that were taking place in India at the end of the eighteenth century under an increasingly confident British rule. This scene at Garden Reach had originally been drawn during the Daniells' stay in Calcutta. But, by the time they came to publish *A Picturesque Voyage*, the old Government House had been replaced with a new one by Richard Wellesley,

the Governor-General at the turn of the nineteenth century. In order to remain up to date, therefore, the Daniells had to rely on other images – possibly an aquatint by James Moffat published in 1805 – for the depiction of the new Government House here.

As a scene of picturesque beauty in Calcutta, Garden Reach was not unique. North of the city, a similar process of managing the landscape to make it conform to European standards took place. Not content with altering the skyline of the city by building a new Government House, Wellesley had appropriated a garden villa at Barrackpore, a military cantonment some fourteen miles north of Calcutta, in order to act as a kind of summer residence for the Governor-General. Richard Wellesley, second Earl of Mornington (subsequently first Marquess Wellesley; eldest brother of Arthur, Duke of Wellington), had travelled to India in 1798 to take up the position of Governor-General in Bengal. In doing so, he had assumed the principal post in Company-controlled India. Laid out on the banks of the river, the house at Barrackpore offered some key aesthetic advantages, and it became a kind of a 'regal palace on fair Hooghly's stream', in the words of Charles D'Oyly.[7] The whole scene presented a kind of sylvan paradise, according to Wellesley's friend Lord Valentia: 'The situation of the house is much more pleasing than any thing I have yet seen', and it was surrounded by 'groves of lofty trees'. Even the water was 'much clearer than at Calcutta, and covered with state barges and cutters of the Governor-General. These, painted green, and ornamented with gold, contrasted with the scarlet dresses of the rowers, were a great addition to the scene.' The final *coup de grâce* was offered by the gardens of Barrackpore Park, which were laid out in the 'English style'.[8] Indeed, so proud was Wellesley of his achievements that

Figure 3.7
Robert Havell, after James Baillie Fraser,
'A View of Barrackpore House, with the Reach of
the River', in James Baillie Fraser, *Views of Calcutta
and its Environs*, part 4, 1824–26 (X 644(10))

he expressly requested that Valentia's travelling companion, the accomplished draughtsmen Henry Salt, stay 'behind me to take views of the place'.[9] Other travellers were almost unanimous in their approval and commendation, regarding Barrackpore as a kind of country estate transplanted to India. Emily Eden wrote that it felt 'something like home ... a beautiful fresh, green park, a lovely flower garden. ... It is much cooler here, and we can step out in the evening and walk a few hundred yards undisturbed.'[10] William Hickey was equally impressed by the grounds, which 'were very pretty laid out with extraordinary taste and elegance, upon different parts of which he [Wellesley] erected a theatre, a riding-house, with probably the finest aviary and menagerie in the world, the latter two being stocked with the rarest and most beautiful birds, and beasts equally uncommon, collected from every quarter of the globe'.[11] The visual depictions of artists like Edward Hawke Locker and James Baillie Fraser replicate these words in their images, offering scenes of order and tranquillity that might just as easily have been in the home counties (Figs 3.6 and 3.7).

Despite the popularity and usefulness of homely, picturesque depictions of the subcontinent, this was not the only way in which the landscapes of India could be represented. European aesthetic notions of the sublime, codified most famously by Edmund Burke in the middle of the eighteenth century, existed to represent the unusual and potentially threatening. For artists and travellers in India, the sublime offered a way of interpreting those scenes that could not easily be compared to reassuringly familiar images of home. It provided a set of compositional strategies and aesthetic devices for representing the unusual places of the subcontinent. One European visitor to 'the grand cave of Cannara [Kanheri]' was adamant that it 'must ever be considered by a man of taste as an object of beauty and sublimity'.[12] And, back in Britain, Joshua Reynolds was aware of the capacity for India to produce the uncommon and the unusual as he commented on the 'barbarick splendour of those Asiatick buildings, which are now publishing'. He felt that they might 'furnish an architect, not with models to copy, but with hints of composition and general effect, which would not otherwise have occurred'.[13]

As the account of the visitor to Kanheri suggests, some of the most 'sublime' places in India for British artists were the examples of rock-cut architecture. Elephanta was the smallest but also reportedly the oldest of the cave temples of western India. Located on an island five miles in circumference, and situated in the inlet between the mainland and the outer islands of Bombay, Elephanta or Gharipuri was named after the large granite formation just outside the main portico of the temple. To many visitors, this extraordinary structure seemed to depict an elephant with a tiger on its back. Elephanta had long attracted those keen to record its stark natural rock outcroppings. The earliest British drawings of the temple were probably done in 1712 by William Pyke, the military cartographer of the East India Company. He paid a covert visit as the Company fought against the Maratha kingdom for control of western India. At the end of the century, James Wales described Elephanta as having 'the grandest and most magnificent scenery I ever beheld, every part, every station presented pictures of astonishing beauty'.[14] Wales would go on to become one of the most important British

Figure 3.8
James Phillips, after James Wales,
'Interior View of the Principal Excavated Temple on
the Island of Elephanta', 1790 (P182)

artists to record these extraordinary formations (Fig. 3.8). Sir Charles Warre Malet, the British Resident at the court of the Maratha Peshwa in Poona (today's Pune), remarked on the extraordinary mixture of natural formation and architectural carving:

> Whether we consider the design, or contemplate the execution of these extraordinary works, we arc lost in wonder at the idea of forming a vast mountain into almost eternal mansions: the mythological symbols and figures throughout the whole, leave no room to doubt their owing their existence to religious zeal, the most powerful and most universal agitator of the human mind.[15]

Although the caves had already excited the attention of scholars and some artists, no complete visual record of them had been made. James Wales changed all of that, offering a series of powerful images that capture the distinctiveness of these features. Born in Peterhead, on the north-east coast of Scotland, Wales followed the path taken by many British artists in the late eighteenth century, seeking permission from the East India Company to go to India. He applied to work in Bombay in 1790, was granted permission on 5 January 1791, and arrived in India on 15 July of the same year. While Bombay was a smaller and less affluent market than Calcutta or Madras for a British painter, Wales was fortunate enough to meet Sir Charles Warre Malet. In addition to

Figure 3.9
Thomas Daniell, after James Wales,
'The Mountains of Ellora', *Hindoo Excavations
in the Mountains of Ellora*, plates 1–3, 1803
(P2890–2)

working for Malet, Wales painted a number of remarkable portraits of the Maratha chiefs and their ministers. But he is perhaps most famous for his detailed studies of the extraordinary rock-cut architecture of western India, and the series of thirty-four caves at Ellora, excavated between the sixth and eighth centuries CE, in particular. The depiction of these caves is indebted to Wales's fortuitous meeting with the Daniells when they visited Bombay in March 1793. He was already engaged on his studies when he met them. They encouraged him to continue his detailed drawings of Indian caves and temples, and later they played an important role in bringing them to the attention of the general public in Britain. Wales took them to see some of the rock-cut temples close to the city, including that on the island of Elephanta. The Daniells did not see Ellora, and Wales himself did not go there until the spring of 1795, after they had left India. Wales intended to produce a major publication on the caves, with engravings after his drawings. While working at the Kanheri cave in October 1795, however, he caught a fever and died before the work was complete. But, through the combined efforts of Charles Warre Malet and the Daniells, James Wales's work reached the public: the Daniells used his sketches, brought back to Britain by Malet, to produce a series of aquatint views of the temples of Ellora, which were published in 1803 (Fig. 3.9). The Daniells' images were intended to appeal to the scholarly as well as the aesthetic impulses of connoisseurs and to offer a thorough and exact sourcebook on Hindu architecture.

Figure 3.10
Thomas Daniell and William Daniell,
'Near Bandell on the River Hoogly',
Oriental Scenery, IV, plate 8, 1797–98
(Tab.599.a/b(4))

TRAVELLING ARTISTS

The meeting between Wales and the Daniells reminds us that it was often by travelling
beyond the confines of the Company's redoubts on the coast that artists – professional
and amateur alike – responded most fully to the variety of sights and scenes in India.
Just as Hodges's art was facilitated by his ability and inclination to move around and
beyond East India Company-controlled territories, the Daniells' expeditions through
the subcontinent provided them with valuable material for their subsequent work.
Their travels indicate the variety of places and experiences that European artists could
sample in India, and show that there was no single response to Indian landscapes
from European artists.

The Daniells landed in India in 1786 and travelled extensively over the next seven
and a half years. Their first long tour took them westwards along the Ganges and
through neighbouring regions, in the footsteps of Hodges. Their route was partly
dictated by the convenience of starting in areas under British control and partly by
their desire to emulate and exceed Hodges. In the end, they went a good deal further, reaching Delhi and even the foothills of the Himalayas. On their way back, they
stopped at Sasaram in Bihar (as Hodges had done seven years before) to visit the
majestic tomb of Sher Shah Sur. After a tour in the south in 1792 – visiting temples
and hill forts that had featured in the recent conflict with Tipu Sultan – the Daniells
called at Bombay where, as we have seen, they met James Wales. They joined him
for a while before beginning the voyage home in 1793. Their numerous oil paintings,

Figure 3.11
Thomas Daniell,
*Rope Bridge over the Alakananda River
at Srinagar, Garhwal*, 1808 (F77)

Figure 3.12
Thomas Daniell,
Landscape in Northern India, c. 1820
(F669)

Figure 3.13
William Daniell,
The Banks of the Ganges, 1830
(YCBA, B1981.25.211)

Figure 3.14
William Daniell,
*Quadrangle of the Jami Masjid,
Fatehpur Sikri,* 1833 (F167)

prints and magnificent aquatints of the six volumes of *Oriental Scenery* (published 1795–1808) constitute a detailed record of Indian architectural history, as well as an extraordinary visual account of their prolonged and profound artistic engagement with India (Figs 3.10–14).

But the Daniells were not the only artists whose travels fired their imagination and whose work demonstrates the impact of Indian topography. George Chinnery worked in India in the first two decades of the nineteenth century. He made his living through the lucrative business of portraiture but his real love was landscape and, throughout his time in the subcontinent, he worked to infuse his images with the local colour of the scenery and sights that he found all around him (Fig. 3.15). William Prinsep was a member of a great British Indian dynasty, being one of the eight sons of John Prinsep, an important East India Company merchant who traded in indigo and chintz in the 1770s and 1780s. As well as being a businessman and banker, William was an enthusiastic artist and traveller (Fig. 3.16). By 1837 he was able to afford a home on Garden Reach, 'adjoining Kyd's dock which ... I had converted into a most pleasant residence with a painting studio commanding the best views up and down the river'.[16]

Another artist with deep ties to the East India Company was James Baillie Fraser. Fraser went to India in 1813 to make his fortune and to rescue troubled family estates in Scotland. When his initial forays in the Calcutta business world ended in failure, he decided to join his brother, William, in the service of the Company. At the end of the Nepal War of 1814–15, William was appointed Commissioner of Garhwal in the Himalayan foothills and his first task was to make an extensive tour. In summer 1815, therefore, the brothers travelled through the hill states: while William negotiated with their rulers, James sketched their dramatic landscapes. Towards the end of the tour,

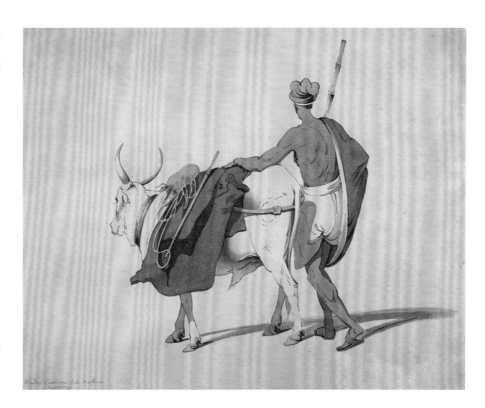

Figure 3.15
George Chinnery,
'Indian Villager with Bullock',
c. 1810–22 (WD353)

Figure 3.16
William Prinsep,
A Village Scene, c. 1820
(WD4028)

Figure 3.17
Robert Havell, after James Baillie Fraser,
'Gungotree, the Holy Shrine of Mahadeo', 1820 (P48)

James struck out on his own, reaching as far as Gungotree, one of the sources of the Ganges, where he bathed in its waters. His account of the incident highlights the deep intellectual and artistic (and, in this case, physical) immersion in the landscape of the subcontinent that many British artists enjoyed:

> The water, just freed from the ice, was piercing cold; and it required no small effort of piety to stay long enough in it for the Brahmin to say the necessary prayers over the pilgrim. … Afterwards, with bare feet, we entered the temple, where worship was performed, a little bell ringing all the time.[17]

Fraser made a sketch of the scene and it was one of twenty drawings made on the tour that were published as aquatints in 1820 (Fig. 3.17). Later in the decade, he published a set of aquatints of Calcutta, where he had returned in a second attempt to become a businessman.

The life and career of Samuel Davis were similarly shaped by the evolving British Empire of the late eighteenth century. Born in the West Indies, Davies was appointed a cadet in the East India Company at the age of eighteen. He spent three years in Madras before taking up a position as 'draftsman and surveyor' on a British mission to the mountain states of Bhutan and Tibet in 1783. Led by Samuel Turner, the mission's purpose was to renew British contact with the court of the Panchen Lama, first established in 1774 by George Bogle. The Tibetan authorities were suspicious, however, and were unwilling to allow a greater number into their territory than had accompanied the Bogle mission. As a result, Davis was left behind in Bhutan and forced to make his own way back to India. In the course of this journey, he made extensive records in watercolour and pencil of Bhutanese architecture and topography, which combine visual accuracy with warm sympathy for the people and places he encountered. In his subsequent account of the expedition, Turner recalled passing the scene shown in Davis's watercolour: 'Punukka is the winter residence of the Daeb Raja, and, as we were informed, his favourite seat: he has lavished large sums upon it' (Fig. 3.18). The gardens, meanwhile, were 'extensive, and well stocked, containing the orange, sweet and sour, lemon, lime, citron, pomegranates, peach, apple, pear and walnut trees'.[18] Like so many others, Davis was also an acquaintance of the Daniells and, in 1813, William Daniell produced six aquatints based on Davis's Bhutan paintings, and a further six in 1816 based on his views of the island of St Helena.

The trend of travel and recording continued well into the nineteenth-century heyday of the Company's power in India. Amateurs and professionals turned to visual images to make sense of the landscapes they were encountering, as a way of transcribing and recording them for posterity, and as a means of interpreting the British – and by extension their own – presence there. Captain Robert Smith (1792–1882) of the 44th East Sussex Regiment – not to be confused with his older namesake, the garrison engineer at Delhi discussed below – had already had a most energetic career in the service of the burgeoning nineteenth-century British Empire before arriving in India in 1828. He had seen action in Sicily, Spain and North America, among other places. Like many

Figure 3.18
Samuel Davis,
The Palace of Punukka in Bhutan, 1783
(WD3271)

soldiers of the period, he was an accomplished draughtsman and devoted much of his leisure to topographical sketching. A series of watercolours survive from his time in India, and depict some of the sites he visited there. These sites – including various places along the course of the river Ganges such as Benares, Chunar, Monghyr and Allahabad – had long been favoured by travelling artists, and Smith followed in some illustrious footsteps. His rendition of the fort at Allahabad, overlooking the important Hindu pilgrimage centre at the confluence of the Ganges and Jumna rivers, was built by the Mughal emperor Akbar from 1582 onwards (Fig. 3.19). But, despite its location in the heart of India, Smith's deployment of the classic picturesque formula renders the scene in familiar terms, as one that might be witnessed along any suitably sinuous river bank.

The work of William Simpson, in the middle of the nineteenth century, demonstrates the continued importance of travel for the visual recording of India as well as the enduring influence of earlier generations of British artists on their successors in the subcontinent. Simpson came from a poor family in Glasgow and was self-educated as an artist. He made his name with his views of the Crimean War and was sent to India by the lithographers Day and Son to depict the events of 1857–8. The mutiny in the Company's Bengal Army, and the wider popular uprising that it sparked, constituted the last act of the East India Company's raj in India: the British government in Westminster hastily assumed the Company's responsibilities as soon as order had been restored. But Simpson's travels in India hark back to earlier artistic encounters with the subcontinent. Simpson wanted to arrive there with a keen visual sense of the kind of subject matter available to the artist. With that in mind, he prepared for his visit by studying the prints of Hodges and the Daniells in the India Office Library. And he interpreted his commission in the broadest possible way. He travelled extensively in India between 1859 and 1862, often in the party of the Governor-General, Lord Canning. But, in early 1861, he struck out on his own to explore parts of central India and Rajasthan. His image of the palace at Amber (today's Amer) was probably worked up later from sketches made on that tour (Fig. 3.20). Simpson paid great attention to architectural details, as can be seen in this watercolour. The palace was built in stages from about 1600 and became the fortified residence of the local rulers before the foundation of the city of Jaipur in 1727. But, despite the apparent realism, there is also an interest in the composition and the rhythms of light and shade. Ultimately, Simpson's project to produce a great book of Indian views never came to fruition. But his ambition to follow in the footsteps of the Daniells and others shows the power of art and travel to shape British representations of and ideas about India.

THE HUMAN PRESENCE IN THE LANDSCAPE

The representation of local architecture, as William Simpson's image reminds us, played a crucial role in many British landscape depictions of India. Thomas Daniell noted, for example, that

> Temples and other sacred structures of the Hindoos occur frequently on the
> banks of the Hoogley; and these buildings, of various forms, and in different

Figure 3.19
Robert Smith,
The Fort at Allahabad, 1833
(WD2087)

Figure 3.20
William Simpson,
The Palace at Amber, c. 1861
(WD3951)

situations, exposed or half concealed among deep and solemn groves, no less holy in the popular opinion, than the edifices they shelter, give an air of romantic grandeur.[19]

But, as well as offering a sense of 'romantic grandeur' or providing aesthetic impact, depictions of indigenous architecture could also be imbued with symbolic resonance. Buildings that represented the religious adherence of the local Indians offered artists a means of commenting on the societies and cultures in their midst. Landscapes that incorporated ruins, on the other hand, could denote the transience of life and the futility of human hubris and ambition.

William Hodges provides an example of the role of local architecture in his depiction of a group of temples at Deogarh in Bihar (Fig. 3.21). The image might have been painted for Augustus Cleveland, the District Collector for the province, with whom he stayed for several months in early 1782. Hodges is fulsome in his description of the scene:

A small village, famous for the resort of Hindoo pilgrims, this being a sacred spot. There are five curious pagodas here, of perhaps the very oldest construction to be found in India. They are simply pyramids, formed by putting stone on stone, the apex is cut off at about one seventh of the whole height of the complete pyramid, and four of them have ornamental buildings on top, evidently of more modern work, which are finished by an ornament made of

Figure 3.21
William Hodges,
*A Group of Temples at Deogarh,
Santal Parganas, Bihar,* 1782 (F396)

copper, and gilt, perfectly resembling the trident of the Greek Neptune. ... At Deogur multitudes of pilgrims are seen, who carry the water of the Ganges to the western side of the peninsula of India.[20]

Hodges's extensive description of the site underlines the fact that visual transcriptions of such scenes were a crucial means of recording them and conveying this information to audiences. But, where the written text gave a detailed description, the painted image captured the novelty and majestic grandeur of the scene for Europeans. In both cases, Hodges emphasises the antiquity and inherent dignity of the buildings and the cultural values for which they stood.

We left Henry Salt sketching the Governor-General's summer residence at Barrackpore. But he and his companion travelled much further afield and saw many more sites of interest in India. Salt had trained as an artist and, in June 1802, he left London and accompanied George Annesley, Viscount Valentia, as his secretary and draughtsman, on Valentia's tour of the East. They visited India, Ceylon and the Red Sea before Valentia was sent on a mission into Abyssinia in 1805. On their return, Valentia wrote a volume of travel memoirs, and Salt published aquatints after his drawings, entitled *Twenty-four Views taken in St Helena, the Cape, India, Ceylon, the Red Sea, Abyssinia and Egypt*, in imitation of the successful Daniells. Valentia and Salt had reached India in early 1803 and, after an extensive tour in the north, they sailed to Ceylon. From there, they visited the south of India, arriving at Rameswaram on 25 January 1804. There they examined the town's principal temple, which was a large complex of structures surrounded by an outer wall and entered through a series of vast pylons or *gopuram* (Fig. 3.22). Valentia was impressed:

> The entrance to the temple was through a very lofty gateway, I should suppose about one hundred feet high, covered with carved work to the summit. It was pyramidically oblong, and ended in a kind of sarcophagus. ... This massive workmanship reminded me of the ruins of Egyptian architecture. ... The whole was well executed, and was the finest specimen of architecture I had seen in the East.[21]

Although Valentia's comment about Egypt is clearly an attempt to interpret strange scenes by relating them to relatively more familiar ones, Henry Salt saw things rather differently. In contrast to Valentia, Salt focused on the liveliness of the scene and succeeded in combining a precise study of the archaeological details of the temple with a representation of its dynamism. Salt is less interested in the passing of time, then, and more interested in the lived experiences of those who moved in and around the buildings.

Just as the temples at Deogarh and Rameswaram represented the vitality and endurance of cultural traditions, so the recording and representation of monuments, mausoleums and ruins could make a powerful statement. On 25 January 1789, as they left the vicinity of the Taj Mahal to move on to Sikandra to draw Akbar's mausoleum, the road there reminded the Daniells of the Appian Way outside Rome, with ruins on

Figure 3.22
Henry Salt,
The Temple at Rameswaram, 1804
(WD1302)

Figure 3.23
Thomas Daniell and William Daniell,
'Cannoge on the River Ganges',
Oriental Scenery, IV, plate 12, 1797–98
(Tab.599.a/b(4))

both sides. The variety of appearance and abrupt shape of the ruins offered a poignant reminder of the transience of all of mankind's efforts in the face of the inexorable march of time. Kanauj, a once flourishing site (Fig. 3.23), moved Thomas Daniell to brood:

> It is impossible to look at these miserable remnants of the great city of Cannoge without the most melancholy sensations, and the strongest conviction of the instability of man's proudest works. ... The plains of India indeed present to mankind many a sad proof of the uncertainty of human glory.[22]

This point was emphasised when the Daniells visited the sixteenth-century mausoleum of Sher Shah Sur in February 1790 during their long sketching tour of upper India (Fig. 3.24). Travellers had long been struck by the stately sandstone tomb of Sher Shah, who had originally come to India to serve the sultans of Delhi but had succeeded in carving out his own independent state in eastern India incorporating parts of Bihar and Bengal, with its capital at Sasaram. With its imposing grandeur, echoes of faded glory, and stark reminder of the transience of existence, the building captured the imagination of many European artists too. The Daniells were certainly deeply impressed by the sober dignity of the tomb, finding that its 'gloomy grandeur ... awakens feelings rather painful than agreeable'.[23]

The engagement with ruins and faded glory could even go beyond individual buildings and encompass whole towns. This seems to have been the case with Sir Charles

Figure 3.24
Thomas Daniell,
*The Tomb of Sher Shah Sur at Sasaram
in Bihar*, 1810 (Tate, T01403)

D'Oyly in a view of Patna taken from an album of sketches containing eighty drawings and eighty-three folios of views in Bengal and Bihar, done between January 1823 and May 1825 (Fig. 3.25). Patna suffered severe economic hardship as a result of the changing business conditions of late eighteenth-century India. Where Calcutta and other large urban centres flourished on account of the increased export business passing though them, many older cities declined. This was the case in Patna, and it was a process witnessed at first hand by D'Oyly. Like Prinsep, he came from an old East India Company family. D'Oyly had returned to India (where he was born) in 1797 and held a number of posts in Calcutta before moving to Patna in 1821 as Opium Agent. He was a prolific artist and published many books with engravings and lithographs from his drawings, including *Indian Sports* (1829) and *Costumes of India* (1830). He even imported a lithograph press to Patna which he ran with the help of local Indian artists. Amongst his many achievements was the formation of an art society in Patna in 1824. In this and other images of Patna, however, the crumbling mosques and great houses seem to reflect the city's economic and political decline.

Figure 3.25
Charles D'Oyly,
Patna City near the Gateway of the Fort, 18 October 1824, 1824 (WD2060)

The career of Colonel Robert Smith (1787–1873) epitomised the way in which visual records were part and parcel of a wider British engagement with the Indian subcontinent. Like John Johnson (discussed in Chapter 1), Smith was a military engineer. But he was also an architect, an archaeologist and a painter. He served during the Nepal War in the early 1810s. Later in the decade, between 1816 and 1819, he spent time in Penang (in today's Malaysia) in order to benefit from the healthier climate there. His views of the island were later published by William Daniell. Eventually, however, Smith returned to India where he was appointed garrison engineer at Delhi. As part of this role, he was responsible for the care of some of the city's greatest ancient monuments. He was involved in the restoration of many of them and he also made extensive records of them in images. After his return to Europe, Smith put his knowledge of Mughal architecture to good, if eccentric, use by designing Indian-style palaces for himself in Nice and Paignton.

One of the most striking records left to us by Smith is his depiction of the fort known as the Purana Qila, where the crumbling edifice offers an imposing backdrop to the two passing elephants carrying their passengers (Fig. 3.26). This complex of buildings was begun by the Emperor Humayun in 1538, but it was completed by the Afghan

Figure 3.26
Robert Smith,
The Kila Kona Masjid, Purana Qila, Delhi, c. 1823
(YCBA, B1976.7.74)

Figure 3.27
Robert Smith,
*Inside the Main Entrance of the Purana Qila,
Delhi,* 1823 (YCBA, B1976.7.73)

chief Sher Shah Sur after his defeat of Humayun. Smith may have used a camera obscura in order to ensure the accuracy of his depiction – the crisp outlines of the buildings suggest this was the case. But it is in the surrounding detail that Smith furnishes a more complex rendition of the scene and provides a sophisticated comment on the history embodied in it. Ultimately Smith offers a musing on history, time and memory to viewers of the image. In another image of the fort, the layers of the building are exposed as being in different stages of stasis and transformation. Its pitted brick façade is a reminder of the passing of time and the futility of human ambition (Fig. 3.27). Meanwhile, however, an Indian soldier in the service of the British and situated close by emphasises the British presence in the city. This element, combined with Smith's role as the garrison engineer and creator of this image, sets the British authorities up as both proprietors and narrators of India's past. Here is the new economic, military and political power – Smith's image seems to suggest – supplanting those that had gone before and represented in the ruins of faded empires that dotted the landscape.

SPECIAL SITES

Throughout this chapter, we have seen how European artists responded to Indian landscapes and the architectural elements they found there. While many places succeeded in exciting curiosity and enthusiasm, a few were particularly prized as sites for artistic recording and aesthetic engagement. Principal among these was the 'Crown of the Palace', the Taj Mahal. It was built by Emperor Shah Jahan as a mausoleum for his favourite wife, Arjumand Banu, called Mumtaz Mahal ('Chosen of the Palace'). When she died in childbirth in 1631, Shah Jahan dedicated the next twenty years of his life to building a suitable memorial for her, eventually completing it in 1653. The grandest of Shah Jahan's architectural projects, it is made of Makrana marble which possesses the most subtle variations of tone. In stylistic terms, the building unites two different architectural traditions as the large bulbous dome is of Persian origin, while the smaller cupolas are indigenous to India.

The Taj Mahal was long regarded as an iconic sight. Writing shortly after its completion, François Bernier immediately recognised it to be one of the wonders of the world. For him, this 'splendid mausoleum is more worthy of a place among the wonders of the world than the misshapen masses and heaps of stones in Egypt'.[24] Thomas Twining, over a century later, was equally enamoured. Although he was less impressed by Shah Jahan's political record as a ruler, he praised him for having 'left to India the most beautiful sepulchral monument the world possesses':

> The beauties of the Taje [sic] more than satisfy all expectation, and more than requite the fatigue and risks of the desert; they leave nothing to desire, to the traveller who beholds them, but the possibility of describing them. But though no pen can describe, and no pencil trace, the beauty of the Taje, its character may be conceived from an expression of the celebrated Zoffany – 'It wanted nothing but a glass case to cover it.'[25]

Figure 3.28
William Hodges,
A View of the Ruins at Agra and the Taj Mahal, 1783
(YCBA, B1978.43.1807)

Figure 3.29
William Hodges,
The Taj Mahal, 1783
(YCBA, B1978.43.1735)

As one of the most accomplished European artists to visit India in the eighteenth century, Johan Zoffany, quoted here by Twining, was well placed to comment on the building's aesthetic and artistic qualities. Another artist who remarked on its iconic global status was Thomas Daniell:

> The Taje Mahel [*sic*] has always been considered as the first example of Mahomedan architecture in India, and consequently, being a spectacle of the highest celebrity, is visited by persons of all rank, and from all parts. This high admiration is however not confined to the partial eye of the native Indian; it is beheld with no less wonder and delight by those who have seen the productions of art in various parts of the globe.[26]

In many ways, it was the work of travelling artists, like Daniell himself, that transformed the Taj into an instantly recognisable monument. When Henry Prinsep visited Agra in 1870, on a business trip from Western Australia, he was immediately impressed: 'A description would give very little idea of its grandeur, situated as it is on the banks of the Jumna, asleep for ever in its large, dark, shadowy gardens.'[27]

William Hodges and the Daniells were among the earliest British artists to see the Taj Mahal, visiting it in the 1780s (Figs 3.28 and 3.29). Like many others, Hodges waxed lyrical in his description:

> It possesses a degree of beauty, from the perfection of the materials and from the excellence of the workmanship, which is only surpassed by its grandeur, extent, and general magnificence. The basest material that enters into this center part of it is white marble, and the ornaments are of various coloured marbles, in which there is no glitter: the whole appears like a most perfect pearl on an azure ground. The effect is such as, I confess, I never experienced from any work of art. The fine materials, the beautiful forms, and the symmetry of the whole, with the judicious choice of situation, far surpasses anything I ever beheld.[28]

In the case of Hodges, however, he reinforced these words by a range of depictions of the scene that so impressed him. In one image, made for his *Select Views in India*, Hodges chooses an all-encompassing and panoramic view which presents the architectural grandeur of the entire scene at Agra (Fig. 3.30). It displays the intricate effects of light, water and atmosphere as Hodges viewed it in the low light of sunset. The foreground shows the river with Indians working on boats in silhouette on it. Agra Fort is reflected in the water with dramatic cloud formations looming behind it. Meanwhile, in the background, the Taj Mahal is displayed amid the brilliance of penetrating light, offering an elegant architectural contrast to the more robust outlines of the fort.

The Daniells reached Agra on 20 January 1789 and pitched their tents 'immediately opposite the Taj Mahal'. They noted in their journal that they spent the entirety of their first day at the site sketching the famous mausoleum and visiting the tomb of Itimad-ud-Daula in the evening. They crossed the Jumna River the next morning and breakfasted with Major Palmer before sketching inside the Taj. Palmer was the British Resident to the Maratha chief Scindia, who controlled the whole area. The following day, 22 January, was also spent drawing the Taj, with Thomas outside in the garden and William focusing on the interior. In the evening, and much to his uncle's consternation, William went up on the dome. They relaxed later by eating the 'apples, pears & grapes of Persia from Major Palmer's table'. The Daniells were similarly employed for the next two days.[29]

The Daniells' time at Agra was explained in a booklet published in 1801 entitled *Views of the Taje Mahel at the City of Agra in Hindoostan Taken in 1789*. It contained two large coloured aquatints along with a descriptive letterpress, as well as a ground plan of the whole area, engraved by James Newtown, with detailed references to various parts of the building. The aquatints were huge. At some three feet across and two feet high, they were larger than those in *Oriental Scenery*. In one, a variety of river boats in the foreground provides a contrast to the monument which is reflected in water. Several Indian figures on the shore – some walking, others reclining and some traders with a camel and an elephant – add a sense of daily life and ordinary activity to the majesty of the scene. The second image (Fig. 3.31) shows the highly ornamental garden that so captivated Thomas:

> The garden view of the Taj Mahal was taken immediately on entering it by the principal gate … whence the Mausoleum, being seen down an avenue of trees, has on first entering a most impressive effect on the spectator. The large marble bason [*sic*] in the centre of the garden with fountains, and those rising out of the watery channel with paved walks on each side, add to the variety and richness of the scene, and give to it that coolness which is so luxurious an improvement to an Oriental garden.[30]

The ornamental fountains play in a pool while Indian figures watch in the foreground as the monument in the middle ground is framed by rows of giant trees and tall thin minarets.

If the Taj Mahal presented a site of singular architectural interest to British travellers and artists, the entire city of Benares (today's Varanasi) offered another site of iconic status. From the earliest days of European contact with the subcontinent, it had excited wonder and awe in those who saw it. The seventeenth-century traveller François Bernier called Benares 'the Athens of India'.[31] Several centuries later, William Sproston Caine thought that it was still 'without question the most picturesque city in India'.[32] When William Hodges exhibited a painting of the city at the Royal Academy in 1788, one reviewer compared Benares with Delft in the Netherlands (Fig. 3.32). But it was also a site where the religious complexity of India was laid bare. Temples, palaces and a monumental mosque jostled for attention. Unlike the calm serenity of the Taj Mahal, then, Benares presented the hustle and bustle of the subcontinent in the context of one of its most ancient and holiest settlements. William Hodges hastened to prepare 'for observing with the utmost attention whatever came within the sphere

Figure 3.30
William Hodges,
*A View of the Fort of Agra on the River Jumna
from the Northeast*, 1783 (YCBA, B1978.43.1802)

Figure 3.31
Thomas Daniell and William Daniel,
'The Taje Mahel, Agra. Taken in the Garden',
*Views of the Taje Mahel at the City of Agra in
Hindoostan Taken in 1789*, 1801 (P928)

of a painter's notice'.[33] Visitors encountered 'a kaleidoscopic crowd' where the number of Hindu 'pilgrims from every part of India' ensured 'every variety of costume, and every stage of dress and undress, grouped under huge straw umbrellas, sitting at the feet of some learned preacher, gazing at holy ascetics, jostled by sacred bulls, crowded in and out of the water, drying themselves with towels, prostrate at the margin telling beads'.[34] For Lady Charlotte Canning, the 'great sight of all was', simply, 'Benares'. This was the only place where she had 'really' felt she had 'seen India' for 'not a trace or touch of anything European exists there'.[35] *The Hindoos*, a popular nineteenth-century guidebook, was equally enthusiastic:

> Benares stands upon the northern bank of the Ganges, where the sinuosity of the sacred river forms a magnificent semicircle, of which its site occupies the external curve. The ground upon which it stands is considerably elevated, particularly towards the centre, from which point the rows of buildings descend in terraces, like the seats of an amphitheatre, to the water's edge.

The whole city was 'studded with innumerable pagan temples' and 'crowned by a lofty Mohammedan mosque', which was 'reflected with all its grandeur in the … face of the Ganges'.[36]

William Hodges's depiction of the city captured the varied and irregular outlines of the buildings and tufted trees. And he enlivened the scene with the inclusion of details such as the figures and boats at the ghats. In addition to the pictorial composition, however, this sustained engagement with the architecture of the city betrays Hodges's interest in its history and his belief in the power of visual depictions to convey more profound truths about the nature of human society and culture. He praised Benares as the ancient seat of Brahmin learning. It was, in his view, perhaps the oldest city in the world and a repository of living history. On his arrival there, he confessed his 'real pleasure' at the prospect of 'being able to contemplate the pure Hindoo manners, arts, buildings, and customs', the more so 'since the same manners and customs prevail amongst these people at this day, as at the remotest period that can be traced in history'.[37] Here was a site where the religious contest between Hindu and Muslim was thrown into sharp relief. Hodges perceived a conflict between what he regarded as the pure, spiritual values of Hinduism and the destructive influence of Islam. This was manifest in the contrast between the sacred Panchganga Ghat in the foreground and the imposing minarets of Aurangzeb's mosque behind. Tradition had it that the seventeenth-century mosque towering over the Panchganga Ghat had been built on the site of an earlier Hindu temple. To this end, most Europeans interpreted its soaring grandeur as a sign of the city's violent past when the Mughal emperor Aurangzeb had allegedly ordered that the Hindu temple be destroyed and replaced by a mosque. The emphasis on the mosque as a decrepit, obsolete relic draws attention to Aurangzeb's fading legacy:

> Nearly at the centre of the city is a considerable Mahomedan mosque, with two minarets: the height from the water to the top of the minarets is 232 feet. The

Figure 3.32
William Hodges,
A View of Benares, 1781 (F94)

building was raised by that most intolerant and ambitious of human beings, the Emperor Aurungzebe, who destroyed a magnificent temple of the Hindoos on this spot, and built the present mosque, of the same extent and height as the building he destroyed.[38]

Hodges reached Benares in August 1781 in the retinue of his patron, Warren Hastings. His studies of the city and its architecture were interrupted, however, by the infamous conflict between Hastings and Raja Chait Singh. As well as its more ancient history, Hodges's view of the city was intimately connected, therefore, with the rise of the East India Company and its increasing political and military dominance in the subcontinent. For some time, Hastings had been attempting to extract additional money from Chait Singh, the Raja of Benares, over and above the dues paid to the Company under treaty arrangements. Chait Singh's refusal to comply prompted the Governor-General to visit the city and to seek redress. The Raja was placed under arrest within his own palace. But his troops came to his aid, rescuing him and massacring the detachment of British sepoys detailed to guard him. As the Raja's troops prepared to attack his small British force, Hastings and his men had to beat a hasty retreat. Hodges was among them, and

Figure 3.33
William Hodges,
View of Part of the City of Benares, 1781
(YCBA, B1978.43.1811)

he was forced to abandon 'the whole of my baggage, excepting my drawings, and a few changes of linen'.[39] Subsequently, British reinforcements were summoned and Chait Singh's uprising was ruthlessly suppressed. By the end of September, Hastings's party was able to return to Benares, and Hodges resumed his dispassionate investigation of the city's antiquities. Quite apart from its importance in the artistic history of Britain's involvement with India, then, this episode was one of the principal matters leading to Hastings's impeachment in 1787.

In addition to his musings on the relative place of different religious traditions in the city, Hodges also offers some local detail to enliven and illuminate the scene. His grey wash, now in the collection at Yale, provides visual information about everyday life in the city (Fig. 3.33). Other travellers also revelled in the pictorial and picturesque details offered by the daily rhythms of the city. Captain Robert Elliott remarked on the ghats of the city:

> The immense flight of steps called the Ghauts of Benares, form a great ornament to the river face of the city. ... Crowds of people come down to wash in, and also to worship, the Ganges. ... The gracefulness of many of the washing figures, the various colours of their dresses, the easy and elegant attitudes in which they stand, and the admirable groups into which they occasionally fall, would form excellent subjects for a painter.[40]

Emma Roberts was similarly stuck by the bustling energy around the ghats:

> The ghauts are literally swarming with life at all hours of the day and every creek and jetty are crowded with craft of various descriptions, all truly picturesque in their form and effect. ... No written description, however elaborate, can convey even a faint idea of the extraordinary peculiarities of a place which has no prototype in the East. ... It is only by pictorial representations that any adequate notion can be formed of the mixture of the beautiful and the grotesque, which, piled confusedly together, form that stupendous wall which spreads along the bank of the Ganges at Benares.[41]

Visual representations of the city did not end with Hodges. Some of the most proficient drawings of Benares made in the early nineteenth century were done by the amateur artist James Prinsep of the Bengal Civil Service. James, like his brother William, had a penchant for making visual records. From 1820 to 1830, James was Assay Master at the Benares Mint. He published *Benares Illustrated in a Series of Drawings* in three parts between 1831 and 1834. A great scholar, deeply learned in Sanskrit texts, Prinsep came to know the city intimately during his time at Benares. His drawings depict not only the ghats, but also the tortuous alleyways of the city, the interiors of the houses, the architecture of temples and palaces, as well as the life of the city – priests reading the Puranas (ancient Hindu texts), crowds waiting for an eclipse of the moon and the great Ram Lila festival (Fig. 3.34). Later in the century, after the demise of the East India

Company, the romance of Benares still attracted artists. Edward Lear was in India from November 1873 to January 1875. Yet his interest in Benares's religious heritage was surely inspired by those who had been there before him. Despite initial difficulties, Lear eventually remarked on how 'truly glad' he was 'to have seen this wonderful place' (Fig. 3.35). His journal recorded how he spent his time sketching the ghats:

> Got a boat, a large one, for no one can have the least idea of this Indian city's splendour without this arrangement. Utterly wonderful is the rainbow-like edging of the water with thousands of bathers reflected in the river. Then the colours of the temples, the strangeness of the huge umbrella and the inexpressibly multitudinous detail of architecture, costume, etc. ... How well I remember the views of Benares by Daniell RA; pallid, gray, sad, solemn. I had always supposed this place a melancholy, or at least a staid and soberly coloured spot, a gray record of bygone days. Instead I find it one of the most abundantly *bruyant*, and startlingly radiant places full of bustle and movement. Constantinople or Naples are simply dull and quiet by comparison.[42]

CONCLUSION

The landscapes of India were as varied as the European artistic responses to them. Some travellers sought the familiarity of home, seeking equivalence and comfort. Certain places, such as the European residences at Garden Reach or the Governor-General's villa at Barrackpore, lent themselves to this kind of interpretation. But the irresistible attraction of India also made its mark on artists. In the representation of Indian landscape scenes, artists were inspired both by what lay before their eyes and by what they drew from their artistic heritage, training and background. Tensions necessarily existed: between the obvious artifice of the picturesque on the one hand, which rearranged or 'improved' subjects and scenes for the sake of both affect and effect, and the desire for truthfulness, accuracy and veracity on the other. Navigating between these two poles defined the distinctive European visual engagement with Indian landscapes in this period.

Landscape views of India were a constant feature of the British encounter with the subcontinent. In this, they reflected artistic tradition and taste back in Europe. But there was another major genre of visual representation that lent itself to describing and depicting the British engagement with India: portraiture. Writing to his friend, Ozias Humphry, the Calcutta-based amateur artist William Baillie lamented the fact that he was not taken serious as an artist in India. This was in spite of the fact that some of his views of the city had been very well received by the critics. Reluctantly, he came to the conclusion that he was wasting his time in 'landscape painting which is unprofitable'. Instead, Baillie was going to try his hand at portrait painting: 'There are but very few judges of a good picture – a likeness is what most people want, and I think I can promise that.'[43]

Figure 3.35
Edward Lear,
A View of Benares, 1873
(WD2330)

CHAPTER 4

People and portraits

The sights and scenes of India were a major attraction for artists. But, as William Baillie's decision to give up 'unprofitable' landscape painting in favour of portraiture demonstrates, recording the people who played prominent roles in the British engagement with India was equally as important and potentially more lucrative for artists.[1] On one level, and before the advent of photography, a portrait offered a way of documenting a person's appearance for posterity or for distant family and friends. For example, on seeing a portrait of the late Benjamin Mee, Lady Russell was sure that his sister, Lady Palmerston, would be 'supremely happy' to possess 'so correct a representation'. The owner of the painting, William Hickey, had a copy made by 'Mr Home, an artist of some celebrity at that time, pursuing his profession in Calcutta', and duly dispatched the original to Lady Palmerston. The noble recipient was suitably impressed by 'this invaluable treasure', which was 'so animated as almost to persuade me whilst regarding the canvas that the lamented object was still in existence'.[2] But portraiture was more than just the capturing of likenesses. Portraits are, as Tillman Nechtman has suggested, visual autobiographies.[3] In the hands of the most skilful artists, a portrait provided a sophisticated means of presenting an image of oneself to the world. In short, portraits are complex historical documents, the deciphering of which opens perspectives on the political, social and economic concerns of the sitters. This was certainly the case in eighteenth-century India. Local rulers attempted to project their political ambitions to the world through the medium of some of the best portrait painters of the day. Wealthy European 'nabobs' sought to capture their political and commercial success in the service of the Company as well as the luxury and opulence of their lives in the East. And Company servants employed artists to convey their achievements and scholarly interests in the subcontinent and its history.

This chapter explores the many facets of the Company's encounter with India through the faces of those who served it, worked with it and opposed it. At its heart, the business of the East India Company was about people as much as commodities. Meeting and persuading people was the key to the Company's activities and its success. Playing politics, cutting a good deal, and having access to the right contacts could make the crucial difference between immense profits and crippling losses. This applied both to the institution and to those who worked for it. The personal encounters recorded in a variety of portraits encapsulate this vital aspect of the British involvement with India. This chapter considers the stories and the people behind these images. Why, for example, were portraits of foreign dignitaries and local Indian rulers sent to adorn the Company's headquarters in London? What about Company men and their families? What do their portraits tell us about their attitudes to India and its people? And what about ordinary Indians, whose lives were affected by the machinations and power politics of the day? What can their (often unnamed) faces tell us about the attitude of British artists and, by extension, the viewers of their images? Portrait artists in eighteenth-century India provide a lens through which we can see the varying ambitions and aspirations of the Indian and European sitters whom they captured in paint.

Detail of Figure 4.27
Thomas Hickey,
Colonel Colin Mackenzie, 1816
(F13)

Figure 4.1
Diana Hill,
William Larkins, 1786
(WD2476)

PAINTERS OF PORTRAITS

The importance of portraiture to the East India Company, or perhaps more accurately to its servants, can be seen in the number of European portrait painters who undertook the long and uncomfortable sea journey to India in order to tap into this apparently lucrative market. The career of Ozias Humphry and his network of artistic contacts across India offer particularly useful insights in this regard. Humphry was among those who marketed themselves as portrait painters to British clientele in India. And in this he was moderately successful. In December 1785, for instance, Humphry received payment from a Captain Edward Brown 'for the account of my ugly face', indicating the sources of patronage that Humphry and his contemporaries relied on.[4]

The example of Humphry also reminds us that there was a wide variety of differ-ent approaches to portraiture. In fact, Humphry was a specialist miniature painter, a kind of portrait that involved 'drawing a perfect likeness in small pictures'. For many people, like Sir John Macpherson, these were the 'most agreeable' kinds of portraits because they had the inestimable advantage of being portable: 'the hand of friendship can always carry them as a remembrance'.[5] A number of women also practised this branch of art. For instance, William Hickey's memoirs recount the story of 'a young

Jewess of the name Isaacs' who had recently 'arrived in Calcutta to exercise the pro-fession of miniature painting'.[6] Diana Hill was another of the many artists who were, according to Thomas Daniell, 'making handsome faces' in Calcutta in the 1780s.[7] She spent some twenty years in India, having applied for permission to travel there after the death of her husband. She had a brother-in-law in Company service in Calcutta, and presumably this was why she had 'adventured across the immense ocean in search of a provision'. In fact, her arrival in 1786 somewhat disconcerted Humphry because she had significant social connections meaning that, unlike him, 'she was powerfully recommended to the leading people' and could presumably expect to profit from this by acquiring commissions.[8] She certainly succeeded in getting business from them. But, as her miniature of William Larkins, the Accountant-General of Bengal, amply illustrates, her extensive contacts were matched by her considerable artistic skill (Fig. 4.1). In her rendition of Larkins's powdered hair, blue coat and frilled white shirt, she managed to convey his graceful bearing and, consequently, something of his eminent social position in Anglo-Indian society. He was an intimate of Warren Hastings, taking charge of his financial affairs after Hastings's departure for England. Indeed, Larkins bequeathed portraits of both Hastings and his successor as Governor-General, Lord Cornwallis, to the East India Company – further underlining the connection between portraiture and power.

It was not just British officials and their families who wanted portraits or for whom portraiture offered an important channel for representing themselves and their relationship with India. Interactions between Indians and Europeans were also brokered through the medium of portraiture. The complex interaction between British forms of representation and its use in mediating the relationship with local Indians is highlighted by another example drawn from the Indian career of Ozias Humphry. Mr MacKinnon wrote to Humphry from Benares, hoping to engage him to paint 'a miniature full-length portrait of Nunco Sing', who was 'a man of some confidence in this place'. MacKinnon, or perhaps the sitter himself, was clear about how Singh should appear: 'It should be in his Durbar or best dress at this season.'[9]

INDIGENOUS RULERS AND THE POWER OF PORTRAITURE

The connection between power and visual representation was something that tran-scended cultures, and the impact and influence of portraiture was recognised not only by the British. As we have seen, the Mughal Empire was the principal political force in India when the East India Company commenced its trading relations with the subcontinent. During the reign of Shah Jahan (1628–58), the Mughal Empire reached its height, absorbing the rich commercial provinces of Gujarat and Bengal. Shah Jahan projected imperial power through elaborate building programmes and architectural schemes. He also harnessed the pageantry of the durbar (*darbar*) ceremony, a kind of imperial assembly that would be rejuvenated and reinvented by the British in the nineteenth century, in the days after the East India Company, for similar ends. But the manipulation of visual spectacle could be achieved on a smaller scale too. The portrait by a now unknown Mughal artist shown in Figure 4.2 is part of that process of presenting the emperor as an august ruler to be revered and respected. Flanked by bearers of ceremonial flywhisks, Shah Jahan holds a ruby while the attendant on the far left holds a tray of precious jewels. Their inclusion here is not coincidental. These objects had both material and spiritual significance for the Mughals. Precious stones advertised the emperor's worldly wealth, but they also offered a parallel to Shah Jahan himself: just as the jewel combined intangible light and tangible matter, so the emperor embodied both spiritual power and worldly influence. The Mughals believed that the emperors were imbued with the radiance of special enlightenment, signified by the 'halo' surrounding their heads in many miniature paintings. The relatively small physical dimensions of this image (305 × 220 mm), and the delicate quality of the artist's work, belie the fact that this is an image about power and position.

Pictures continued to play an important role in the representation of local Indian rulers in subsequent decades. Like their Western counterparts, Indian rulers acknowledged the power of visual images to influence and to affect those who saw them. When he was at Delhi, the King of Persia, Nadir Shah, had two portraits of himself painted. The circumstances of their creation and their ultimate destination – the walls of East India House in London – give us an insight into the power, influence and aspirations of the man being depicted. As a political personality, Nadir Shah played an important role in eighteenth-century India and in hastening the downfall of the Mughal Empire. With its capital at Delhi and under the control of emperors like Shah Jahan, the Mughal Empire endeavoured to control the subcontinent. But the death of his son, Emperor Aurangzeb, in 1707 marked a sharp decline in its fortunes. By the mid-eighteenth century, the empire was crumbling. Regional enemies – such as the Sikhs, Jats and Marathas – damaged the Mughal economy and its revenues, but a humiliating defeat by the Persians in 1739, led by Nadir Shah, accelerated its downfall. This defeat on the plains near Delhi proved disastrous for the Mughals, and highlighted their rapidly diminishing authority. The major provinces under Mughal control were increasingly restive for autonomy and it encouraged local zamindars (landholders) to rise up against the emperor. Historians have long debated the importance of this power vacuum for the extension of East India Company control. But, as the commissioning, acquisition and display of the portrait shown in Figure 4.3 illustrates, Nadir Shah was recognised (both by himself and by others) as an important figure in the recent history of the subcontinent.

Although the technique is Persian, the composition is heavily influenced by the European models that must have been familiar to the artist, possibly through the circulation of European prints in India. As a result, the painting demonstrates the kinds of cultural cross-fertilisation that increasingly came to characterise late eighteenth-century India. In a further instance of the overlap and intersection between local Indian and British Company power, one of the two portraits commissioned by Nadir Shah was presented to the British Governor of Madras in 1740. This was more than just a diplomatic gift – it served to keep the King at the forefront of the British authorities' calculations. His painted presence reminded them of his political and military presence in the subcontinent. Depicted wearing a scarlet tunic and a high cap (*tahmazi*)

ornamented with a jewelled aigrette, the King cuts a suitably regal figure. And the portrait continued to exert an influence after his death. It was eventually acquired by Henry Vansittart, the Governor of Bengal (1760–67), whose son passed it on to the East India Company in 1822. The directors ordered it to be deposited in the Company's library. The presence of the King in a London reading room served to remind anyone who saw it of the complex system of brokerage required to preserve power in the subcontinent. It illustrated the visual opulence and splendour of the local Indian rulers who played such a major part in determining the nature and success of Company rule there.

EUROPEAN ARTISTS AND INDIAN SUBJECTS

As we have seen in the example of Ozias Humphry, one of the consequences of the East India Company's presence in India was the encouragement it gave to artists to come to India. The life and work of one of the first British professional artists to do so, Tilly Kettle, gives us an insight into the ways in which art – and portraiture in particular – was intimately intertwined with the rise of the East India Company and its involvement in Indian politics and society. A brief summary of Kettle's career illustrates the breadth of his activity in India and the impact of the subcontinent on his work. In August 1768 Kettle petitioned the Company to travel to Bengal to work as an artist. Permission was granted the following month and he set sail aboard the *Nottingham* on 24 December 1768, carrying letters of recommendation from Laurence Sulivan, an influential director of the Company. Kettle was the first professional painter to travel to the subcontinent following the Company's rise to power in the wake of the Battle of Plassey and the granting of the *diwani* (see Chapter 2). He arrived in Madras in May 1769 and spent two years there. His patrons were composed of local Indian dignitaries, Company merchants and army officers who worked together to cement and extend British control in the region. In an indication of the continued importance of Indian rulers, Kettle's most significant portraits during his time in Madras were those he did for Muhammed Ali Khan Walla Jah, the Nawab of Arcot. Kettle painted a group portrait of the Nawab with his five sons, which he exhibited at the Society of Artists in London in 1771.

Meanwhile, Kettle had made his way to Calcutta by late 1771. He stayed here briefly before travelling on to Faizabad, apparently at the invitation of Shuja-ud-Daula, the Nawab of Awadh, whose portrait he painted on several occasions. During this time Kettle took an Indian *bibi*, or mistress, with whom he had two daughters. He arrived back in Calcutta in early 1773, where he stayed for a further three years. His return to this hub of British power is not difficult to explain: Calcutta offered a greater range of opportunities for patronage from some of the most important figures in the British administration. Among Kettle's numerous commissions were portraits of Sir Elijah Impey, first Chief Justice of the Supreme Court of Bengal, and Warren Hastings, the Governor-General, whom he painted on at least three separate occasions. Like many of the artists whom we have met in this book, Kettle probably never intended his stay in India to be permanent. In March 1776 he left India on board the *Talbot*, bound for London, arriving there in mid-November. But India remained central to everything

Figure 4.4
Tilly Kettle,
Shuja-ud-Daula, Nawab of Awadh,
Holding a Bow, c. 1772
(YCBA, B1976.7.48)

he did. Finding it difficult to attract new clients in London, he relied on the network of patrons that he had established in India. Ultimately, the lure of recreating past successes (and perhaps happier days) in India proved impossible for him to resist and, in the summer of 1786, Kettle set out overland for Asia. By July, he is recorded as having reached Aleppo, but sadly he never reached his destination. Kettle is thought to have died some time before the end of 1786, possibly in the desert on his way to Basra, although the exact date and circumstances of his death are unknown.

The attraction of India for Kettle, and his willingness to risk (and ultimately lose) his life to return, are easier to understand when we consider his achievements there. Kettle's time in Awadh (or Oudh), with its two great cities of Faizabad and Lucknow, was perhaps the most artistically important and productive phase of his career. Situated on the fertile plains irrigated by the Jumna and Ganges rivers, the region was at the centre of an area of intense interest, first to the Mughals and then to the East India Company. Its large population of 20 million people constituted an important market in itself. The region which, during Kettle's time in India, was ruled by Shuja-ud-Daula, was also at the crossroads of the crucial trading routes between Delhi in the interior and Murshidabad and Calcutta on the coast. Shuja had ascended to power in 1754 and gradually expanded his realm, annexing the richer parts of surrounding states. But he made one fundamental error: in 1763 he joined forces with Mir Kasim of Bengal against the British. Shuja's decision to oppose the East India Company was understandable: he saw how it operated and wanted to confine its influence to Bengal. But his ploy did not work out in practice. Defeat at the Battle of Buxar in 1764 led to a long and debilitating relationship with the Company, which would eventually lead to the annexation of the province by the British in 1801.

Kettle's portraits of Shuja-ud-Daula, whom he painted on at least eight occasions, convey something of this situation. In one of these, the Nawab is shown in three-quarter length, holding a bow in his right hand, while a canopied garden pavilion and a group of Indian attendants occupy the background (Fig. 4.4). Proud, dignified and physically powerfully, Shuja-ud-Daula was highly educated and possessed of charm and a keen wit. His administration was well run and he himself was a skilful diplomat. Kettle's portrait captures the dignity of the ruler. In another image, known through a version made by an Indian artist in 1815, a bespectacled European artist is shown in the foreground, working on a group portrait on the easel in front of him (Fig. 4.5). Shuja and his sons are depicted standing under a cusped archway with richly decorated columns, while the European artist is seated on an ivory chair, busily recording the family ranged before him. The willingness of Indian rulers like Shuja-ud-Daula to recognise the value of European portraits in helping to forge political alliances is an interesting example of the centrality of art to the process of Company control in India (as well as to its role in recording that rise to power).

Further south, the work of George Willison also illustrates the way in which European artists reflected the changing circumstances and balance of power in India. Perhaps encouraged by the example of Tilly Kettle, Willison spent six years in India from 1774 to 1780. He worked in Madras, where he charged the considerable sum of £120 for a

Figure 4.5
Indian artist,
*Tilly Kettle Painting a Portrait of Shuja-ud-Daula, Nawab of Oudh,
with Ten Sons*, c. 1815 (Victoria & Albert Museum, IS.5-1971)

full-length portrait. Willison was not just a portrait painter. He also turned his hand to historical and religious subject matter. His altarpiece for St Mary's Church in Fort St George, for example, depicted the Last Supper and borrowed extensively from Raphael's widely known cartoon of the same subject. As with many of his peers, however, Willison's most lucrative work was not for European traders or officials but rather at the court of the local ruler, the Nawab of Arcot. As we have seen, the Nawab was painted by Tilly Kettle during his brief sojourn in Madras. For his part, Willison painted Muhammed Ali Khan Walla Jah, Nawab of the province of Arcot in southern India, on numerous occasions. Willison was nothing if not commercially astute: he doubled his fees for the Nawab and, according to his friend Ozias Humphry, received between £17,000 and £20,000 from the Nawab and his second son. Willison is also known to have possessed an enormous fortune in jewels acquired in India, which he sold off in 1793.

Willison painted six full-length portraits of the Nawab and his family in 1774 and 1775 alone. The work of European artists like Willison was a central feature of Muhammed Ali's drive to secure his realm. The son of a soldier and adventurer from the north, Muhammed Ali needed to establish himself in a land where Muslims were few and adherence to an ancient Hindu cultural heritage strong. He built palaces and mosques, and he commissioned portraits. Several of the full-length portraits painted by Willison in 1774–5 were dispatched to people and institutions that the Nawab wanted to secure as allies: George III, Warren Hastings and the directors of the East India Company in London all received his likeness. Willison produced two further full-length portraits of Muhammad Ali a few years later, as well as one of his second son and another of his young grandson, all four of which were sent to the exhibition at the Society of Artists in 1777. Despite his close connection with the Nawab, Willison did not let personal sentiment get in the way of business. In the same year that his portraits of the Nawab of Arcot hung on the walls of the Society of Artists, Willison also worked for the Nawab's enemy, the Raja of Tanjore.

Willison's popularity with the Nawab is easy to understand from the serene and majestic portrait of the prince in the collection of the India Office Library (Fig. 4.6). The Nawab stands on a patterned carpet on a verandah with a large pilaster and balustrade behind him. The composition is not original: it borrows unashamedly from Tilly Kettle's portrait of 1770, simply reversing the pose. Like Kettle's earlier image of the Nawab, the sitter is shown wearing exquisite robes of fine silk, draped around his body in multiple layers. The strings of pearls and other jewels, and the great sword that he holds in his left hand, accentuate the impression of majesty, power, substance and wealth that the Nawab sought to convey to viewers. The weapon, deadly but decorative, seems to embody the idea of a venerated but potentially violent and despotic Eastern potentate. Nevertheless, it is clear that for Muhammad Ali the Kettle and Willison portraits helped to present him as the epitome of the aristocratic and rightful ruler of his realm: wealthy, discerning and wise. But his taste for expensive paintings also led Muhammad Ali into the clutches of British creditors in Madras: their expensive loans entangled the Nawab in a debilitating spiral of debt and ultimately reduced him to the status of a dependent pensioner of the East India Company.

If the careers of Tilly Kettle and George Willison were forever defined by their time in India, Johan Zoffany already had an international reputation for excellence before he followed in their footsteps. Characterised by Warren Hastings as 'the greatest painter that has ever visited India, unless Alexander brought Appelles with him', Zoffany was certainly one of the most illustrious artists to travel to the subcontinent in the eighteenth century.[10] But reputation could only get him so far, and he too sought the patronage of wealthy Indians, and of the court at Lucknow in particular. Zoffany was born in Frankfurt am Main and initially made his name in London, painting the great theatre aficionado David Garrick, among others, on his way to acquiring the royal patronage of Queen Charlotte. The fact that he fell out of favour with the Queen has sometimes been used to explain his departure for India. However, given the fresh fields of patronage and subject matter being opened up to European painters by the advance of the East India Company, it is just as likely that Zoffany travelled to Asia in search of fresh experiences and new sources of wealth.

Zoffany sailed for India in March 1783 and arrived at Calcutta on 15 September. He was well connected and was immediately taken up by the Governor-General, Warren Hastings. He was energised and enthused by the richness and variety of the Indian scenes that he met, recording the landscapes, their crumbling buildings and their twisted trees in his sketch books. His stock-in-trade, however, was portraiture. In India, Zoffany painted both life-size portraits of individuals and small conversation pieces of British families. Some of the latter were indistinguishable from the kinds of commissions that he had executed in Europe. Others, however, included certain recognisably 'exotic' elements: Indian attendants; a brilliance of colour, light and atmosphere; and 'oriental' settings and backgrounds.

Following an intensely productive stay in Calcutta, where he painted many of the elite of the British community there, Zoffany moved on to Lucknow. There was a large population of Company officials and private merchants here, subsisting on the huge profits to be made from breaking into the trade and wealth of the surrounding province. Zoffany spent much of his time in India in Lucknow. And it was here that he painted some of his most brilliant pictures of European life in the subcontinent and of Indian princes and nobles. He made friends with the Swiss colonel Antoine Polier and the French general Claude Martin, both cultivated men who had entered the Nawab's service. In one of his finest Indian works, Zoffany depicted himself painting in the background, while his friends are apparently deeply immersed in the study of the pictures and manuscripts with which they are surrounded.[11] In contrast to this contemplative image, the other side of life in Lucknow is illustrated in *Colonel Mordaunt's Cock Match*, which he painted for Warren Hastings.[12] This extraordinarily vivacious and dynamic image shows Indians and Europeans mingling on the easiest of terms at the court of a Muslim prince. But it was in and around the court of the Nawab himself where Zoffany really wanted to make his mark. Where Kettle had initially succeeded in the 1770s, Zoffany sought to emulate a decade later. He got his chance in May 1784 when Hastings commissioned him to paint a portrait of the Nawab, Asaf-ud-Daula, who had succeeded his father, Shuja-ud-Daula, in 1775 (Fig. 4.7).

Hastings's interest in having a portrait of Asaf-ud-Daula reminds us that the Company and its officials were not entirely benign bystanders in the evolution of European–Indian relations. Under Asaf-ud-Daula, Awadh's dependence on the British became more and more conspicuous, progressively chipping away at both the Nawab's treasury and his pride. The original 'subsidiary treaty' which had been signed in 1765 following the Battle of Buxar (1764) compelled the ruler to pay for the Company's troops deployed in his territories. The sums demanded were huge: they may have constituted up to half of the total revenues of the realm. Unsurprisingly, the Nawab quickly fell into arrears. As he became increasingly desperate to service the debt, he borrowed heavily from local bankers and wealthy rural magnates. And Asaf's troubles did not end there. His position was constantly imperilled by the machinations of his ministers, who played politics with successive British residents and East India Company officials. For those who disliked Asaf and regarded him as shifty, degenerate and untrustworthy, a luxurious portrait such as this one by Zoffany only added to the impression of a man seemingly addicted to frivolity. Yet Asaf's apparent deceit might also have been a deliberate ploy on his part to try to hide the true level of his revenues from the British and to maintain his independence. Whatever the true meaning of Asaf's actions, the

Figure 4.8
Tilly Kettle,
An Indian Dancing Girl,
c. 1772
(YCBA, B1981.25.385)

work of artists like Tilly Kettle, George Willison and Johan Zoffany illustrates the way in which British political, economic and artistic engagements with the subcontinent were often filtered through indigenous rulers and power brokers.

Of course, not all of the artists who came to India were able to, or interested in, painting grand portraits of local Indian rulers. They found other ways of interpreting, representing and recording the Indian people whom they encountered during their time in the subcontinent. Indeed, even in the work of the 'court' artists that we have considered, there was sometimes room for the diurnal and the everyday. For example, Tilly Kettle's image of an Indian dancing girl reflects the tastes of the court at Lucknow (Fig. 4.8). But it also captures something of the ordinary workings of daily life in these places. Dances in the northern Indian style, Bharatnatyam, were a favourite entertainment for the Mughal aristocracy and proved of particular fascination to European travellers in search of the exotic. Kettle continued and extended this interest in other work. He painted a series of genre pictures of everyday life, which he exhibited in London in 1772, while a suttee scene showing a woman preparing for self-immolation on her husband's funeral pyre was probably displayed at the Free Society of Artists in 1776.

As with his grander portraits, Kettle's example was taken up by later artists and travellers. Ozias Humphry's miniature work did not prevent him from making lively pastel sketches of Indian servants (Fig. 4.9). As we have seen, Thomas and William Daniell played a crucial role in recording the landscapes of India. But their extensive travels in search of the sights of the subcontinent also brought them into contact with a variety of its people. Some of their sketches are simple records of the several dozen servants, palanquin bearers and watchmen whom they employed on their various expeditions. At other times, they focused on specific 'types', such as the sketch of a Nayar, one of the warrior ruling caste of the Malabar coast, today's Kerala (Fig. 4.10).

Figure 4.9
Ozias Humphry,
Indian Women, Calcutta, December 1786, 1786
(Add MS 15961, f.2)

HOOKKABURDAR.

Nº 1.

Geo. Chinnery delt et aqua f.

Figure 4.11
Etching after a drawing
by George Chinnery,
Hookkaburdar, 1807
(G.45/6, plate 56)

There were more systematic attempts at recording the faces of ordinary Indians. During his time in Madras, George Chinnery got involved in a project designed to depict local scenes and people. The *Madras Courier* reported in November 1806 that 'proposals for publishing monthly a work to be entitled the "Indian Magazine and European Miscellany"' were being advanced. It proceeded to give details:

> Mr George Chinnery, as Joint-Proprietor of the work, will furnish an etching monthly. The first number will exhibit a view of Madras, from the beach; and every succeeding publication will contain either a landscape from nature or figures illustrative of the character, and occupations of the natives; to be accompanied by a description of the plate.[13]

Chinnery contributed nine sketches between February and October 1807, including a number of 'character' sketches that managed to preserve the dignity of the subjects. Chinnery's plan was probably inspired by similar images depicting street traders, such as the 'Cries of London', which were popular genre subjects in Britain at the time. With the advantage of being on the spot, artists like Humphry and Chinnery sought out their picturesque equivalents in India (Fig. 4.11). In relation to the 'water women' (Fig. 4.12), for instance, Chinnery commented:

> They are particular from their persons being often of a very fine shape; and their elegant manner of carrying the pots of water on their head does not fail to strike every observer – the simplicity of the dress they wear, and the style in which this is put on, gives a great similarity of appearance in them to the Antique figures and they are, generally speaking, very Picturesque.[14]

Arthur William Devis was another peripatetic artist who made his way eastwards in the wake of rising British interest in Asia. His initial travelling plans had very little to do with India. His father, who was also an artist, obtained a commission for his son as the draughtsman aboard the *Antelope*, a messenger ship commissioned by the East India Company to sail to China. Sending artists on voyages of exploration was common at the time. Devis was to be paid 100 guineas to make maps of the islands in the South China Sea. On the outward journey he was wounded in the chest and jaw when the *Antelope* stopped off the coast of New Guinea to trade with the locals who had paddled out to meet them.[15] The *Antelope* eventually reached Macau in June 1783. After repairs had been made, it started on the return journey. In early August, however, the ship ran aground on an uncharted coral reef close to a group of islands now known as Palau. All but one of the crew survived and Devis, who evidently had salvaged his drawing materials, recorded the construction of a smaller ship made from the wreck of the *Antelope*. Captain Henry Wilson, in command, described the extraordinary adventures of the crew, in which Devis figured prominently, as they made the acquaintance of the 'Pelew' islanders and assisted them in conquering the neighbouring islands. Devis's studies of the King of Pelew and his wives were used subsequently to illustrate George Keate's *Account of the Pelew Islands* (1788), and several of Devis's Pelew landscapes and portraits were exhibited at the Royal Academy and the British Institution between 1796 and 1807.

In many ways, then, it was through chance and necessity, as much as through planning, that Devis equipped himself to record ordinary Indian lives. Following his adventures in South-East Asia, Devis made his way to Calcutta in September 1784, where he received a number of lucrative portrait commissions. But, even then, he was unable to obtain sufficient patronage to support himself. So, while travelling in search of potential clients, he began collecting material for an ambitious series of paintings depicting 'the arts, manufactures, and agriculture of Bengal', which was to be engraved in colour and dedicated to the orientalist Sir William Jones (see below). Devis found rich material in Santipur, sixty miles north of Calcutta, for example. He travelled there

Figure 4.13
Arthur William Devis,
Grinding Corn, c. 1792–95
(YCBA, B1981.25.747)

Figure 4.14
Frans Balthazar Solvyns,
'A Jellee-a, or Fisherman',
The Costume of Hindostan, 1804
(142.g.15)

during the cold weather of 1792. Santipur was the centre of the Bengal muslin industry and it gave Devis the chance to study artisans and craftsmen at work. He worked up drawings and made studies of local industries and occupations. The *Calcutta Gazette* announced that 'Mr Devis is at present at Santipur busily engaged in the execution of his paintings from which the engravings of the arts and manufactures of Bengal are to be taken'.[16] Only four of the engravings were ever published, but the thirty oil paintings that Devis made provide a unique record of life in rural Bengal, combining loosely painted, delicately coloured landscapes, a naturalistic figure style and finely observed still-life elements (Fig. 4.13).

Some of the most important representations of ordinary Bengali people were made by Frans Balthazar Solvyns (Fig. 4.14). He trained in Antwerp as a painter, sketcher and engraver, and lived in India from 1790 until 1804. Although he was credited with painting shipping particularly well, Solvyns's enduring importance rests on his comprehensive survey of Indian communities, costumes and customs.[17] With the encouragement of William Jones, the great sponsor of intellectual engagement with Indian religion, culture and society, Solvyns declared his intention to produce some 250 coloured etchings, to be issued in parts between 1793 and 1799. These etchings would serve to illustrate 'the character, customs and manners, the persons, and dresses, of the inhabitants of Hindostan, their implements of husbandry, manufacture, and war – their modes of conveyance by land and water – the various sectaries of religion with their peculiar ceremonies, and the appearance of the face of the country'.[18] They were finally published, with bilingual text, as *Les Hindous, ou description de leurs-moeurs, coutumes, et ceremonies* in Paris, from 1808 to 1812.[19] Solvyns's images cover an extraordinary range of everyday activities and give an insight into Indian life beyond the courts and the palaces of its rulers: varieties of occupation and dress, Hindu ascetics and religious festivals, musical instruments, vehicles and boats, even methods of smoking. The images of Chinnery, Devis and Solvyns do not offer us named Indian sitters. But, although they may not confirm to the strict definition of portraits, these images provide intriguing and original perspectives on the lives of ordinary Indians at a time when their country was undergoing momentous changes.

EUROPEAN PATRONS: ASSIMILATION AND ASPIRATION

Despite the importance of Indian princes and people in their work, most European artists who travelled to the subcontinent expected to paint for European patrons. Even here, though, there was significant room for diversity and variety. In some cases, portraits of Company men and their families demonstrated the assimilation of Europeans to Indian cultures and ways of life. In other instances, however, they reflected a desire to remain aloof from the Indian sights and scenes around them.

The portrait of the Palmer family offers us a fascinating case study of the kinds of cross-cultural connections and personal relationships that enlivened the eighteenth-century British engagement with India (Fig. 4.15). The identity of the artist is not entirely clear: both Johan Zoffany and Francesco Renaldi have been suggested. While it lacks the visual splendour and accomplishment of Zoffany's other work, its unfinished state

Figure 4.15
Johan Zoffany,
Major William Palmer with His Second Wife,
the Mughal Princess Bibi Faiz Bakhsh, c. 1786
(F597)

may be explained by the fact that it was painted between Zoffany's arrival back in Lucknow, in April 1785, and Palmer's departure for Calcutta in July. The focus of the picture is Major William Palmer who is depicted in the centre of the family group. Palmer had entered the East India Company's army in 1766, becoming aide-de-camp to Warren Hastings in 1774. The image shows the British officer in a red military tunic, while the women and children that surround him are dressed in cream-coloured clothes of various hues. The group is located on a red carpet in a courtyard at night, with palm and plantain trees completing the scene. To the left sits Begam Faiz Baksh, a princess from Awadh, with whom Palmer lived for thirty-five years and to whom he left his house and lands when he died in 1816. Two of their children, William and Mary, stand on either side, while the baby, Hastings, is in her arms. The painter has enlivened the scene, seeming to capture a particular moment in time as Palmer leans towards her and affectionately looks down on his children. The two other seated women are probably Faiz's sisters, while the women standing on either side of the main group are ayahs (children's nurses). Although the portrait of the family posed on the terrace of their palace is unfinished, it still conveys a sense of domestic and interracial harmony.

It is worth pointing out that European patrons seeking somebody to paint their portrait did not always look to a European artist, or even to European forms of pictorial representation. This is the case with an image of Warren Hastings painted by an unknown Mughal artist (Fig. 4.16). Hastings's decision to have himself depicted like this may be explained by his deep immersion in the cultures of India. When he first arrived in Calcutta in September 1750, his prospects were just like those of Company servants of previous generations. He had to learn how to order textiles and check their quality, the mainstay of the Company's business in eighteenth-century India. And he had to know how to deal with local Indian traders and middlemen. Hastings's first appointment was at Cossimbazar (sometimes spelled Kasim Bazar), a major centre for procuring silk. This background, together with the linguistic and cultural skills that it helped him to acquire, explains Hastings's close engagement with India and its people. He dealt directly with Indians in a way that would be unimaginable and thoroughly objectionable to his successors. And this close relationship is evident in some of the portraits of Hastings that survive from his time in India. For example, the sketch for a painting by Johan Zoffany in 1784 shows him speaking, presumably in Urdu, to a Mughal prince without an interpreter. The portrait illustrated here, painted by a now unidentifiable Mughal artist, is equally suggestive. It shows Hastings in European court dress, but also seems to give a sense of the kinds of cultural interchanges between people that existed in the period and that were actively fostered by Hastings during his time as Governor-General.

Figure 4.16
Mughal artist,
Warren Hastings in European Court Dress,
c. 1782 (Or. 6633, f. 67a)

Figure 4.17
Indian artist of the Delhi School,
*A European Smoking a Hookah
(possibly Sir David Ochterlony)*, c. 1820
(Add. Or. 2)

Figure 4.18
John Thomas Seton,
*Lieutenant General Sir Eyre
Coote*, 1783 (F7)

An even more striking example of this occurs in a portrait of (almost certainly) Sir David Ochterlony (Fig. 4.17). In the early decades of the nineteenth century, Ochterlony became the first British Resident at Delhi. He was active in defending the city against the resurgent Marathas in 1804, and achieved considerable and significant military successes against the Gurkhas (1814) and during the Pindari War (1817–18). In spite of (or perhaps because of) his activities in defence of the interests of the East India Company, Ochterlony assimilated to his surroundings and became a celebrated character in Delhi. He is said to have lived in the 'Indian style'. An indication of what this might have involved is given by a local artist in this image. Ochterlony is depicted in Indian dress at home, watching a nautch (a dance display) while smoking a hookah. Although the practice among Europeans in India of publicly adopting indigenous forms of dress was commonplace in the eighteenth century, it had become increasingly unusual by the nineteenth, although lightweight coats and other comfortable garments were acceptable for informal wear indoors. The images of Palmer and Ochterlony represent a way of life that had begun to fade by the early nineteenth century. Although Company officials still engaged intensely with India in pursuit of their business and political interests, they became less interested in representing this in their portraits. In the work of many British artists working there, India played a marginal role as they concentrated on conveying the successes, aspirations and ambitions of their patrons.

John Thomas Seton was the son of a Scottish gem engraver who went to India in 1776. Although few authentic works by him survive, Seton did gain some notable commissions. Among these was the portrait of Sir Eyre Coote, which was commissioned in 1783 (Fig. 4.18). The frailty of the full-length figure depicted by Seton may be an indication of the physical state of the general, who died in April that same year, 1783. Coote leans on a table strewn with quill pens and documents. Accoutrements like these – suggestive of Coote's importance as a leader and administrator – were the standard props of portraitists everywhere, and the sparse background betrays no hint of the setting or context in which Sir Eyre made his name. The portrait of a seated Warren Hastings is slightly more revealing but even here India is only tangentially present (Fig. 4.19). Known through a mezzotint, the Governor-General is shown holding a letter, suggesting his active role in administering the business of the East India Company.

Figure 4.19
Engraving after a painting (1784) by John Thomas Seton, 'Warren Hastings', 1785 (P796)

Figure 4.20
Johan Zoffany,
*Colonel Blair with his Family and an
Indian Ayah*, c. 1786 (Tate, T12610)

While Seton's portraits of Coote and Hastings depicted the public sphere of men at business, portrait artists were also increasingly engaged to fulfil more domestic and personal requirements. As we have seen in the case of William Palmer, the family or group portrait – the conversation piece – was a fashionable way of representing one's closest relations, family and friends. Here again, however, Indian themes could be conspicuous by their relative absence. For example, in a classic conversation piece Johan Zoffany depicts Colonel William Blair and his family on the verandah of their house in Cawnpore (Fig. 4.20). Despite the inextricable connection of the people shown here with India and the East India Company, the image is remarkable for its limited reference to the subcontinent. The extreme left-hand side of the painting offers the merest sliver of a view on to their garden. On the right of the main group, the younger of the two Blair daughters, Maria, is pictured with a young Indian girl wearing a red and gold shawl and holding a cat. Behind the group, three landscapes on the wall represent Indian scenes. But these visual clues as to the location of the scene are very much subsumed in a thoroughly domestic scene that barely acknowledges the family's presence in India or Blair's connection to the Company. Although Zoffany was, as we have seen, a skilled master of recording the local sights and scenes around him, he excludes the Indian context entirely in his portrait of Sir Elijah Impey, the Chief Justice of Bengal (Fig. 4.21). The judge dominates the enormous canvas with his physical presence and active gestures. In the background, a symbolic sword of justice rests against a chair, while a mace of office is also present. Impey's left hand leans on a table piled high with legal texts, while his right hand extends in a gesture of benevolence and authority. The brilliant scarlet of his robes and the dynamic tension of Impey's pose further enliven the portrait, creating an image of justice embodied. But it is one that is almost entirely denuded of any sense of the local context in which Impey worked.

Figure 4.21
Johan Zoffany,
Sir Elijah Impey, Chief Justice of Bengal, 1783
(P694)

The taste for European portraiture among the Calcutta elite is expressed in the beautiful pendant pair showing Sir Robert and Lady Chambers, painted by Arthur William Devis in the mid-1780s (Figs 4.22 and 4.23). We last met Devis when he was depicting the common folk of upstate Bengal. But he relied on clients such as the Chambers couple to sustain him in trade, and would go on to garner some high-profile commissions in Calcutta. For example, following the military victory over Tipu Sultan, Devis charged the extraordinary sum of £2,530 for his portrait of the Governor-General, Lord Cornwallis, receiving two of Tipu's sons as hostages. At least three versions of the event were completed; the largest, measuring over four metres in length, includes over sixty portraits of officers and Indian dignitaries. In this pair, however, Devis's work is much more domestic and understated. Lady Chambers was the daughter of the sculptor, Joseph Wilton, and a noted beauty. Samuel Johnson betrayed grudging

Figure 4.22
Arthur William Devis,
Sir Robert Chambers, c. 1789
(YCBA, B1981.25.335)

Figure 4.23
Arthur William Devis,
Lady Chambers, c. 1789
(YCBA, B1981.25.336)

admiration for Sir Robert who had, Johnson thought, 'with his lawyer's tongue, per-suaded [her] to take her chance with him in the East'.[20] She is shown seated in a chair. The dense foliage and huge tree behind her reveal a palm tree and Muslim tomb in the far distance. By contrast, Sir Robert is shown indoors, resplendent in his deep scarlet judicial robes, his right arm resting on a table. The interior is probably that of the New Court House at Calcutta. The portraits do not entirely exclude India, but the references are carefully modulated and managed. This balancing act was something that most portrait painters had to struggle with when they took on Indian commissions. Thomas Hickey, to whom we now turn, was no different.

THOMAS HICKEY: A CALCUTTA PORTRAIT PAINTER

The example of Thomas Hickey alerts us to the contexts and constraints within which artists, and portrait painters in particular, worked in India. Hickey was born in Dublin in May 1741. His early artistic training followed the usual pattern: trips to Italy with extended stays in Rome and Naples. Hickey subsequently set up a practice in Bath, perhaps the most important location for portraitists in the British Isles after London. But, as we have seen, the increasing British involvement in India in the second half of the eighteenth century opened up an entirely new field of subject matter and potential patronage to artists like Hickey. As a result, he applied for, and received, permission from the East India Company to go to India in March 1780. However, Hickey needed more than the mere acquiescence of the Company's directors in order to attract important commissions. He set about gathering endorsements from colleagues and friends. On 6 July, Sir Joshua Reynolds – perhaps the pre-eminent British artist of the day – wrote on Hickey's behalf to Warren Hastings. Reynolds recommended 'a very ingenious young painter' who wished 'to make a trial of his own abilities' in India.[21] This intervention by a widely respected and influential contemporary painter was obviously tremendously helpful for Hickey. But it also underlines the way in which Indian travels and sojourns affected the general art world in Britain.

The endorsement of Reynolds counted for nothing, however, when the vessel on which Hickey was sailing to India was attacked and captured by a combined fleet of French and Spanish ships. The last years of the War of American Independence spilled over into European waters and it was only because of his status as a non-combatant that Hickey eventually succeeded in arguing for his release. Perhaps this experience curtailed his enthusiasm for long-distance travel because, instead of proceeding to India, Hickey went to Lisbon instead. For three years, he ran a profitable practice as a portrait painter in the city. But India evidently still attracted him, and he left Portugal and arrived at Calcutta in March 1784. Hickey met with considerable success there, living in a large handsome house in the most fashionable part of the city. He later moved on to Madras before another short sojourn in Calcutta and then a voyage home.

His connections with the subcontinent endured. Hickey returned for the last time to India in early 1798. He arrived as the fourth and final of the Anglo-Mysore Wars was reaching its denouement with British Crown and Company forces involved in the tussle with Tipu Sultan. When Tipu was killed and his capital at Seringapatam taken, Hickey found himself the only portrait painter on the spot and his services were urgently sought. He made a series of much admired chalk drawings representing some fifty-five British officers. These sketches were intended as preparatory drawings for a series of large history paintings covering the events and occurrences of the last Mysore war. Although this project never materialised, portraiture took up most of Hickey's time. In 1799 he painted a full-length portrait of Richard Wellesley, the Governor-General, for the Exchange at Madras (now at Apsley House in London). A series of sixteen Indian dignitaries for Government House in Calcutta was completed in 1805. And, like many of his contemporaries, Hickey was gainfully employed in painting portraits of British residents in India. His experiences in India were so wide-ranging and eclectic that when, in 1804, a history of the East India Company was being mooted, Hickey unsuccessfully proposed himself as the historical and portrait painter to the Company. He moved to Calcutta in May 1807, where he remained for five years before returning to Madras, where he settled with his elder daughter until his death there in 1824.

This short sketch of Hickey's life cannot do justice to the range of commissions that he completed. Examples of his work demonstrate the diversity of personalities, interests and concerns that occupied British artists when they came to India. A brief consideration of some of Hickey's work amply illustrates this. Towards the end of his first stay in India, Hickey painted John Mowbray, a Calcutta-based merchant (Fig. 4.24). He depicted Mowbray seated, with his servant standing on one side and a *banian*, or merchant, on the other who holds a typical Indian commercial ledger. Such *banians* were drawn from traditional commercial castes. As with portraits anywhere, the objects included and the composition of the picture play a vital role in conveying the wider message. Seated and relaxed, Mowbray looks every inch the wealthy and successful merchant that he aspired to be. The map on the wall displays Bihar and Tibet, suggesting the remit of the Company's trade and indicating the sources of commodities like cloth, saltpetre and Himalayan wools.

A slightly deeper investigation of the image and its sitter reveals further information about the workings of the Company at this time. Mowbray was a partner in the Calcutta-based private trading firm of Graham, Mowbray and Skirrow. The presence of private trading firms in the centre of what was, ostensibly at least, an East India Company monopoly concession, shows how complex things had become. As British trading and business interests in Bengal had grown, the Company's charter and its regulations had struggled to keep pace. Company servants were prohibited from engaging in trading items with Europe privately. As a result, and in order to augment their relatively modest salaries, many writers invested in the Asian or 'country' trade. This trade was managed by Indian agents who also carried on their own private trade along with that of their employers. Huge fortunes were available to both Indians and Europeans by this means. Litter wonder then that papers and books litter the scene in this image of John Mowbray. This was big business. And yet an air of confident calmness pervades the scene. This is a busy man but one who is in firm control of his extensive business affairs.

Figure 4.24
Thomas Hickey,
John Mowbray, Calcutta Merchant,
c. 1790 (F638)

Figure 4.25
Thomas Hickey,
Purniya, Chief Minister of Mysore, c. 1801
(YCBA, B1973.1.22)

If Hickey's image of Mowbray conveyed the complexity of the economic and commercial situation, his portrait of *Purniya, Chief Minister of Mysore* suggested some of the most important features of the transition to British rule in the subcontinent (Fig. 4.25). The composition and placement of the figure is distinctly European, while the architectural background is classical. Yet, this is an image about cultural connections and crossover, and it shows the ways in which alliances could change rapidly in the maelstrom of late eighteenth-century Indian politics. Initially, Purniya had worked for Tipu Sultan in Mysore, where his competence and organisational skills had marked him out and facilitated his rise to prominence. He kept the revenues coming in and the various arms of government running smoothly. He rose to become head of the Revenue and Military departments in Tipu's administration. But in 1799, during the

Figure 4.26
Thomas Hickey,
*Lieutenant-Colonel (later Major-General)
William Kirkpatrick with his Assistants,*
c. 1799–1800 (National Gallery of Ireland,
Dublin, NGI.1860)

final Anglo-Mysore War, the British bought him off and he offered only token resistance as their armies bore down on Seringapatam. As a reward for betraying his master, Purniya was given a position as chief financial officer (*diwan*) in the administration of the restored Hindu Wodiyar rulers of Mysore. In this role, Purniya played an important role in reconstructing the kingdom and transforming it into a client state of the East India Company. As part of the process of presenting Purniya in his new guise, Hickey includes a variety of symbols and gestures that represent justice and administrative integrity. There is no reference to Purniya's complicated employment history, just a beautifully finished image of an important statesman.

On first appearance, Hickey's full-length portrait of William Kirkpatrick might suggest a similar concern with the military and political aspects of British rule in India (Fig. 4.26). Kirkpatrick enjoyed a successful army career in India, serving as military secretary to Richard Wellesley and as Persian interpreter to the Commander-in-Chief of the British forces. But there is, perhaps, an additional layer of meaning here. The officer is presented in uniform with assistants, guards and interpreters. In the background is St Thomas's Mount in Madras. Kirkpatrick was a mild-mannered man with a gift for oriental languages and an extraordinary knowledge of Indian law and customs. The range of his activities, alluded to obliquely in this image, is a reminder that the Company's commercial and political interests in India inspired a variety of responses. These were represented even more forcefully in Hickey's portrait of Colonel Colin Mackenzie (Fig. 4.27). The depictions of Kirkpatrick and Mackenzie introduce another important aspect of the British engagement with India in the period that found expression in a number of contemporary portraits: the interest in Indian history, religion and culture.

LEARNING AND CULTURE

Colin Mackenzie's career mirrored that of many other Company servants. He was born in the Outer Hebrides in 1753 and arrived in India in 1783, where he served with the Madras Engineers. Knowledge of the landscape and topography of the regions under its control was a vital asset for the East India Company, and Mackenzie's work played a crucial part in acquiring it. He was appointed engineer and surveyor in Hyderabad and, for much of the 1790s, he worked to create a detailed map of the Deccan Plateau in central India. He was diligent and methodical. To aid him in his work, Mackenzie often gathered a small team of assistants, including several Indians, mostly paid by himself. As well as helping him in his surveying work, they introduced Mackenzie to 'Hindu knowledge'. He wrote that it was only after meeting a young Brahmin scholar, Kavali Venkata Boriah, that he found the means of combining historical research with surveying work in order to build up a more complete picture of the lands through which he was travelling. Such was his gratitude that Boriah's family was remembered in Mackenzie's will.

Mackenzie's endeavours were not just confined to military cartography. His working methods and experiences in central India led him to contend that effective government relied on a profound engagement with the surroundings in which one worked

Figure 4.27
Thomas Hickey,
Colonel Colin Mackenzie, 1816
(F13)

and through which one travelled. As a result, he advocated undertaking comprehensive surveys of all the territories controlled by the East India Company. Mackenzie's belief in the power of knowledge and empirically based research informed all of his subsequent work. He travelled across northern India in 1814, viewing the Himalayas, taking copious notes and collecting manuscripts, coins and inscriptions. He compiled a wealth of histories, descriptions and oral testimonies. He collected works on Hindu and Muslim holy men, and descriptions of towns and villages. Mackenzie claimed credit for discovering the distinctiveness of Jainism, the usefulness of inscriptions (particularly to understand land tenures) and the significance of ancient stones, trophies and burial mounds. His research was published in a number of learned journals. He amassed objects and documents that could be used in understanding and interpreting the subcontinent and its people. Mackenzie's collections, which comprise thousands of inscriptions, tracts and artefacts, are among the most important sources for the study of Indian history, recording otherwise unknown or neglected periods.

Hickey's portrait of Mackenzie was painted to commemorate a specific occasion: his appointment as Surveyor-General of India in 1816. But it goes some way to encapsulating Mackenzie's rich and comprehensive engagement with Indian topography, history and society throughout his time in the subcontinent. One of Hickey's last and finest pieces, the painting was produced when the artist was seventy-five years of age. Mackenzie is depicted with three Indian assistants. One of them, Kistnaji, is holding a telescope, suggesting Mackenzie's commitment to empirical research, careful observation and scientific methods for advancing knowledge about Indian topography. To the left, a Jain *pandit* (a scholar and teacher) carries a palm-leaf manuscript underlining Mackenzie's interest in the stories, histories, folklore and traditions of the people and areas in which he worked and travelled. The background of the picture is dominated by the huge tenth-century CE statue of the hero-king Bahubali, located at Shravan Belagoa, the holiest Jain pilgrimage site in southern India. Its inclusion serves a twofold purpose: it further highlights the antiquity and rich history of the country; and it had a personal association for Mackenzie as he was probably the first European to measure and record the site.

The cultural and intellectual engagement of Colin Mackenzie, so evident in his life and encapsulated in Hickey's portrait, was mirrored in the careers of other British and Company officials in India. From the days of Warren Hastings, Company merchants and military men had been encouraged to think beyond the pages of the business ledger or the walls of the barrack room. Indeed, Hastings himself had deployed portraiture to display his learning. He commissioned Joshua Reynolds to paint him holding documents written in Persian. The image acts as a summary of his programme for education and cultural cooperation in India. Hastings had recently drawn up a proposal for a 'Professorship of the Persian Language' at Oxford in which he suggested that knowledge of Asian languages was not simply a tool for ruling in Asia but that it would also create awareness of the rich cultures of India, about which many people in Britain seemed unaware or uninterested. Ultimately, he believed that a greater dialogue between the cultures would facilitate a 'reconciliation' of 'the people of England to the

natives of Hindostan'.[22] Hastings's interest in Indian cultures was deep. But perhaps the most intense and profound engagement of any eighteenth-century European with India was that of Sir William Jones. Jones inspired others around him and, in 1784, he founded the Asiatic Society of Bengal. This institution provided a forum for discussion and debate. Lectures were delivered and papers were read on 'oriental' subjects, both cultural and scientific, which were then published in the Society's journal, *Asiatick Researches*. The most distinguished early contributions were Jones's own, most notably his work on the Sanskrit language. In this, he built on the earlier research of Charles Wilkins, whose achievements Jones readily acknowledged and whose translation of the Bhagavadgita had appeared in 1785. Yet again, a painted image – by Arthur William Devis – was deployed to highlight and convey these aspects of Jones's career (Fig. 4.28).

Jones's interest in scholarly and scientific pursuits was a natural one for the son of a distinguished Welsh mathematician. Jones's father was a friend of Sir Isaac Newton and Edmond Halley, but William's interests turned out to be rather more literary in nature. He was fascinated by oriental languages, their roots and origins, long before he went to India. And his keen mind was put to the service of opening up these languages for his compatriots: as well as establishing his international reputation, Jones's *Grammar of the Persian Language* (1771) was used in the training of East India Company writers. In March 1783 Jones got the opportunity to experience India at first hand when he was appointed as a judge in Bengal. He arrived in Calcutta later that year and made his mark on his new environment almost immediately. By establishing the Asiatic Society of Bengal the year after his arrival, Jones facilitated the process of uncovering a vast sphere of knowledge and learning to East India Company employees and many others besides. He was the mainstay of the institution, being responsible for over a third of the papers read to the society during the years of his presidency. The society's journal, *Asiatick Researches*, published papers upon a vast range of subjects, many of which Jones wrote himself. Subjects as diverse as anthro-pology, archaeology, astronomy, botany, ethnology, geography, music, literature, physiology, languages and inscriptions, mythology and religion found a home in the pages of *Asiatick Researches*.

Perhaps Jones's most celebrated contribution to scholarship about India is his work on Sanskrit. On 2 February 1786, only about six months after he had begun to study the language, he presented the 'Third Anniversary Discourse' to the Asiatic Society. In it, he offered a startling idea: the notion of linguistic connections and relationships across continents. Here was a revolutionary – some might even say subversive – view of language that discovered the shared heritage and similarities of the languages spoken by the European rulers and their Indian subjects. Jones had laid the foundations of all modern comparative historical linguistics. And the importance of his work did not go unnoticed at the time. The reviewer of the third volume of *Asiatick Researches* in 1797 in the *Monthly Review* thought that the scholarship contained in its pages and conducted by members of the Asiatic Society formed 'a monument more durable than brass, which will survive the existence and illustrate the memory of our eastern dominion'. The author of the review was in no doubt:

After the contingent circumstances to which we owe our present preponderance in that country shall have ceased to operate, and the channels of Indian knowledge and Indian wealth shall have again become impervious to the western world, the Asiatick Resarches will furnish proof to our posterity, that the acquisition of the latter did not absorb the attention of their countrymen to the exclusion of the former; and that the English laws and English government, in those distant regions, have sometimes been administered by men of extensive capacity, erudition, and application.[23]

The apparent juxtaposition set up by this reviewer – between knowledge and learning on the one hand, and power and wealth on the other – did not necessarily hold true, of course. In fact, far from being polar opposites, they were closely connected. But Jones's contribution to the advance of scholarship is unquestionable, and it is something that Devis attempted to capture and convey in his portrait.

Devis did not shrink from presenting a realistic view of his subject. The somewhat care-worn figure of the forty-seven-year-old Jones is in sharp contrast to the debonair young man painted by Joshua Reynolds twenty-five years earlier. But the most significant thing in the image is not Jones's countenance, demeanour or pose but, rather, the object with which he is depicted. Jones is seated with a figure of the god Ganesha in his guise as patron of learning. The importance of this inclusion can be better understood by consulting Jones's own writing. To illustrate his essay 'On the Gods of Greece, Italy and India', Jones had cited Ganesha as being comparable to the Roman god Janus:

The God of wisdom in Hindustan, painted with an elephant's head, the symbol of sagacious discernment. ... All sacrifices and religious ceremonies, all addresses even to superiour [sic] Gods, all serious compositions in writing, and all worldly affairs of moment, are begun by pious Hindus with an invocation of Ganesa; a word composed of *isa*, and governor or leader, and *gana*, or a company of deities.[24]

The inclusion of a statue of Ganesha in close proximity to Jones was not coincidental. The physical juxtaposition between the two in Devis's image served to underscore their symbolic connection.

CONCLUSION
William Jones was an intellectual colossus who bestrode a host of European fields of learning about India. But, as we have seen throughout this chapter, portraiture served all kinds of purposes for a variety of people. Portraits did not necessarily have to be about the great and the good. They could also be used to commemorate and to exhort emulation in others. The East India Company's reliance on shipping can be discerned from the portrait of John Dean. In 1743 the directors of the Company asked Willem Verelst to paint a portrait of Dean, the only survivor of an incident that struck right at the heart of the Company's activities. The notorious storms and rough seas in the southern stretches of

Figure 4.29
Willem Verelst,
John Dean, Shipwrecked Mariner, 1743
(F19A)

the Indian and Atlantic oceans were universally feared by sailors who had to pass through them on their way to and from Asia. These seas claimed numerous ships over the years. The Company's ship *Sussex* suffered a similar fate in 1738, on her return voyage from Canton. It was crippled by a storm off the Cape and all but sixteen hands abandoned ship. But those who remained somehow managed to sail the ship to Madagascar. The ill-fated *Sussex* proved impossible to refit, however, and the ship fell to pieces, with just enough time for five sailors to escape the stricken vessel. The sailors' ordeal continued: all of them except John Dean fell sick and died before they could be rescued. The tale of the *Sussex* is a salutary one and reminds us of the dangers and perils faced by East India Company sailors and ships as they went about their business.

As a subject to adorn the Company's headquarters, the breaking up of a ship on a rocky coast was unlikely to be highly prized. But the Company did perceive an opportunity in the tragic tale, and one to which the power of portraiture was put. The Company, therefore, focused on the story of John Dean and commissioned a portrait as a celebration of his bravery and endurance in the face of almost insurmountable odds (Fig. 4.29). Although the *Sussex* foundered, and its cargo and most of its crew were lost, Dean was warmly received by the Court of Directors and given a pension and a copy of the portrait. The placement of the original, in a prominent position in East India House in London, was a powerful visual reminder of the power of endurance and fortitude in the face of adversity – precisely the kinds of virtues that the Company valued in its captains, sailors and servants on land. Its location in East India House also reminds us of the way in which the Company used art and visual representations as a means of promoting itself and its activities. It is to that subject that we turn in the next chapter.

CHAPTER 5
Patronage

When he published his *Select Views in India* between 1785 and 1788, William Hodges dedicated this group of aquatints to the East India Company. Hodges was one of the most important European artists to travel in the subcontinent in the eighteenth century. And the forty-eight images that comprise his *Select Views* were similarly influential, acting as a point of reference for subsequent views of India by European and Indian artists alike. But his dedication is equally as illuminating in revealing the crucial role played by the East India Company in bringing visual representations of India to the eyes of audiences in Europe. And, as we have seen in the case of Hodges and Warren Hastings, the backing of individuals connected with the Company could also be pivotal in supporting the work of artists. Throughout the period discussed in this book, the East India Company and its servants were central to the artistic endeavour of Europeans in India. Their patronage resulted in the commissioning and purchasing of works of art, bringing into existence visual representations of India that would not otherwise have been made.

Individual patrons, often with deep connections with India, were instrumental in encouraging artists. They bought pictures from their favourite artists and transported objects, images and other items of material culture from India for display in Britain. Even in the architecture and design of their British homes, these people conveyed their links with, and interest in, the subcontinent. Thomas Daniell painted a composite image, *View of Hindoo and Moorish Architecture*, for the Indian Room in the London mansion of the collector Thomas Hope. He was also invited by Major Sir John Osborne, a retired army officer, to design an oriental garden folly for his house at Melchet Park, on the Hampshire–Wiltshire border. As might be expected from somebody who had travelled extensively in India, Daniell based his concept on 'the chastest models of Hindu architecture'.[1] Presumably this knowledge was one of the key reasons behind Osborne's decision to employ Daniell in the first place. The temple's exterior was decorated with religious figures representing the principal incarnations of the Hindu deity Vishnu. But, rather than filling the temple with Indian gods, Osborne placed a bust of his mentor, Warren Hastings, inside the edifice.[2] These were not isolated examples. Indeed, in his *An Enquiry into the Changes of Taste in Landscape Gardening and Architecture* (1806), the landscape gardener Humphry Repton prophesised that Britain was 'on the eve of some great future change in both these arts [gardening and architecture] in consequence of our having latterly become acquainted with scenery and buildings in the interior provinces of India'. According to Repton, the designs published by Daniell, Hodges and other artists 'produced a new source of beauty, of elegance and grace, which may justly vie with the best specimens of Grecian and Gothic architecture'.[3]

Those artists preparing to travel to India knew that they needed to attract the eye of wealthy patrons there in order to make the trip worthwhile. Before he left Britain, Ozias Humphry spent much of his time gathering recommendations from friends and contacts that he hoped would help him to garner patronage in India. Sir Robert Palk was willing to introduce him 'to Mr Vansittart if he goes to India', and Sir George Yonge did likewise to Sir John Dalling in Madras.[4] The success or otherwise of an artistic sojourn in India was dictated by the likelihood of obtaining commissions from patrons of the arts. When Humphry arrived in Calcutta, for example, he was perturbed to learn of death of 'Mr Wheeler', the resignation of Warren Hastings and the return of Sir John D'Oyly, upon whose patronage he had been relying. In order to mitigate the potential damage to his business prospects, Humphry took the step of writing to various people asking to be recommended to John Macpherson, the then governor.[5]

Although individual patrons were clearly important, and their support could materially affect the livelihoods of European artists in India and Britain, the most significant 'patron' of the day was the East India Company itself. The Company was not just a commercial entity, whose impact was felt on the dining tables or in the haberdashery shops of Europe. It also played a significant role in mediating the relationship between India and Europe through its encouragement and support of the visual arts. This process was perhaps most obvious in the Company's impressive headquarters on Leadenhall Street in London. East India House embodied, in many ways, the Company's activities and successes in the Indian subcontinent. In addition to acting as the beating heart of a great global corporation, the building was a site where art and architecture were employed in the service of the Company's public image. Willem Verelst's portrait of the shipwrecked mariner John Dean (discussed in Chapter 4) was just one of many canvases exhibited inside this imposing edifice (Fig. 4.31). The architectural features and interior decoration of the building, as well as the artwork hanging on its walls, encapsulated and conveyed the Company's self-image and understanding of its role and successes in India. The very fabric of the building projected the impression of an economically sound and flourishing company. The exterior was freighted with symbols that exuded stability, gravity and longevity. And the interior was similarly embellished. From the sculptures adorning the Sale Room and the landscapes displayed in the Directors' Court Room to the portraits of formers governors hanging in the Finance and Home Committee Room, the Company carefully presented its pedigree for employees, visitors and passers-by alike.

This chapter explores the different ways in which views of India – from landscapes and portraits to maritime scenes and symbolic renditions – entered the cultural consciousness of eighteenth- and nineteenth-century Britain. It considers the practicalities involved in 'picturing India' for British audiences. The discussion begins by examining the role of individual patrons and concludes by considering the impact of the Company as an institutional patron. By analysing the circumstances surrounding the patronage, collecting and display of images, we can gain greater insight into the impact and influence of picturing India on British art and society in the days of the East India Company.

INDIVIDUAL PATRONS

Individual servants of the East India Company played a major role in bringing representations of India to Britain. Their time in India, living with its people and among its landscapes, often inspired a profound interest in the country and a desire to bring something of it back to Europe when they eventually returned. In some instances, this was the historical art of India: religious sculptures, architectural fragments, or archaeological remains. At other times, these Company men looked to local, indigenous artists to make contemporary representations of Indian life. And at yet other times, as we have seen, these individuals turned to European artists working in the subcontinent to represent the people and places of the subcontinent.

Historians have recently become much more aware of the multiple avenues that existed in early modern Britain for displaying one's Indian interests and connections through domestic art and architecture. Many fragments of Hindu sculpture were shipped to Europe on Company ships, where they were incorporated into the collections of connoisseurs. Those with strong East India Company ties might amass entire collections of Asian art and sculpture to be displayed in their homes. Valentines Mansion in Essex, owned by the ship captain and owner Charles Raymond, was described by Sylas Neville in 1785 as 'the small but neat box of the retired East India captain'.[6] Visitors to the house often referred to it as a 'cabinet of curiosities'. Raymond was certainly in a good position to accumulate such evidence of Indian and Asian art: he may have collected objects on his own travels aboard Company ships. In his subsequent career, as the principal owner of many East Indiamen, Raymond also stood to receive gifts from the captains and prospective captains of his vessels. Raymond certainly presented his neighbour, the antiquarian Smart Lethieullier of Aldersbrook, with a piece of sculpture composed of hard, dark marble brought back from the island of Elephanta near Bombay. And Charles Raymond was not unique. Nathaniel Middleton housed his collection of Indian miniatures and Persian manuscripts at his residence, Town Hill Park in South Stoneham near Southampton. And there were even more obvious ways to advertise one's Indian connections. In 1793 James Forbes constructed an Indian temple in the gardens of his estate in Middlesex. It was surrounded by a group of statues that he had brought back from South Asia which were, somewhat erroneously, 'said to be the only specimens of Hindoo sculpture in England' at the time.[7]

As these examples demonstrate, the representation of India in eighteenth-century Britain was not just confined to two-dimensional images. Collecting and displaying material culture was widespread among Company men as a way of advertising their interest in, and connection with, the subcontinent. Robert Clive brought a large collection of Indian ceremonial objects to Britain, while Warren Hastings returned with a great deal of ivory furniture. Indeed, this European interest in Indian religious artefacts, weapons, furniture and other curiosities probably inspired local Indian craftsmen to respond to this demand. By the late eighteenth century, these kinds of objects were being made specifically for sale to Europeans with the idea of sending them to Europe:

> Things we never see, except when we buy them for the purpose of sending them home. ... The palm leaf or ivory fans, the curiously carved ivory balls, and the talc paintings, on the mantle-piece – the large umbrella, the sola hat, the long spear, and the battle axe, in the lobby – the leopards' or tigers' skins on the landing place of the stairs.[8]

The example of Thomas Twining gives us a further insight into the eclectic tastes of these Company men, as well as the sheer range and variety of the objects they shipped to Europe. Before he left India in 1795 for health reasons, Twining commissioned 'small, but very exact, models of the principal machines and instruments used in the agriculture and manufactures of India' from 'an ingenious workman of Santipore'. These 'machines' included a model of an Indian plough and 'an excellent one of an Indian loom, with the threads upon it, executed with remarkable precision and neatness'. But Twining's interest in commemorating his time in the subcontinent did not end there. Keen 'to increase my collection of objects relating to India', Twining bought oil paintings 'by an able European artist' at auction. The subject matter of the works gives another example of the eclectic tastes and interests of people collecting images of and from India:

> One represented an elephant with a howdah upon his back, kneeling to be mounted; another exhibited two or three zuz, a small leopard of elegant form, used in hunting the antelope. There were muzzled and had collars round their necks and were led by their attendants like greyhounds to the chase.[9]

Although Twining is silent about their impact, these images would certainly have caused a stir and inspired curiosity in drawing rooms in eighteenth-century England.

Many objects were transported from India to Europe. But, as the example of Twining highlights, the portability and cultural cachet of images made them an easily collectible and much sought-after category of art object for the returning European eager to demonstrate his wealth and cultural sophistication. And it was not just European artists who benefited from the interest of Company servants in representing aspects of Indian life and nature. Individual patrons also turned to the indigenous artists active in major commercial and political centres like Calcutta, Lucknow and Delhi. For example, Sir Elijah and Lady Impey were enthralled by the natural history of India and, in the late 1770s, they employed several Indian artists to paint pictures of the local flora and fauna. Three of these artists – Sheikh Zain-al-Din, Ram Das and Bhawani Das – hailed from Patna. Like many other artists – Indian and European alike – they came to Calcutta looking for work among East India Company officials and their families. The Impeys' collection, which they subsequently brought back to Britain, played a major role in adding to the sum of European knowledge about the natural history of the subcontinent. Thomas Pennant, in his *View of Hindustan*, published in 1798, recorded the generosity and learning of 'Sir Elijah Impey and his lady'. They gave Pennant 'the most liberal access to their vast and elegant collection of drawings, made with such fidelity on the spot'. In an interesting example of the way in which images of India produced by indigenous artists could be disseminated in Europe, the Impeys gave Pennant 'permission to have several copies made by my paintress, Miss Stone, taken from the most curious subjects of their cabinet'.[10] William Roxburgh, the Company botanist in Madras, had similar recourse to indigenous Indian artists. He commissioned and supervised some 300 drawings by Indian artists, which were subsequently engraved in Roxburgh's *Plants of the Coast of Coromandel* (published 1795–1820). He continued this pattern of patronage when he moved to Bengal. When

Maria Graham visited the Botanic Garden in Calcutta in 1810 she described how 'Dr Roxburgh obligingly allowed me to see his native assistants at work, drawing some of the more rare of his botanical treasures; they are the most beautiful and correct delineations of flowers I ever saw'. Mrs Graham was keen to give credit where it was due: 'Indeed the Hindoos excel in all minute works of this kind.'[11]

In addition to their interests in natural history, the Impeys also collected miniatures painted by Indian artists. This format was popular, as we have seen, among both European and Indian patrons. And as British influence extended to northern cities, this gave many Company men the opportunity to add to their collections of miniatures.[12] For instance, Sir Elijah's role in the Company's judicial system in India took him to Lucknow and Murshidabad, giving him access to the Indian artists who painted for the local nobility there. Perhaps the most important patron for any artist in late eighteenth-century India was the Governor-General in Calcutta. We can see the tastes of one of them, Richard Wellesley, the Earl of Mornington (later Marquess Wellesley), in the 'Wellesley Album', now in the British Library.[13] This collection consists of seven groups of drawings (totalling 138) mounted and bound into a single volume. It depicts the monuments, manners and customs of the subcontinent. The album was acquired together with a much larger collection consisting of twenty-seven volumes of drawings delineating plants, birds, quadrupeds, insects and fishes of India and the East Indies. The drawings were almost certainly made specifically for Wellesley, and acquired on loose sheets from a number of different artists. Among these are sixteen drawings of picturesque scenes with Indian monuments done by a Calcutta artist between 1798 and 1804. These include a free rendering of William Hodges's 'A View of the Ruins of Part of the Palace and Mosque at Futtypoor Sicri', which had been published as Plate 11 in his *Select Views in India* in the late 1780s (Fig. 5.1). The close visual correspondence between these works highlights the brisk circulation of images in late eighteenth-century India. This example suggests that Calcutta artists in the 1790s were aware of William Hodges's *Select Views* and used these images to make further sets of landscape drawings depicting Mughal monuments for the British.

Of course, in addition to indigenous Indian material culture and artwork, individual European patrons also evinced a strong enthusiasm for contemporary European representations of India. This interest ranged across a wide variety of visual art, from landscapes and portraiture to scenes of maritime activity and historic events. We have already seen how important the support and patronage of Warren Hastings were to William Hodges. But Hodges did not just work for Hastings. For example, his depiction of a group of temples at Deogarh in Bihar (see Chapter 3) was probably painted for Augustus Cleveland, the District Collector for Bihar, with whom Hodges stayed for several months in early 1782. At the sale of Cleveland's effects in February 1794, there were twenty-one oils by Hodges, suggesting Cleveland's interest in, and encouragement of, Hodges's work. And this phenomenon was not confined to India. The majority of James Wales's work would have been lost or forgotten had it not been for the diligence of his friend Charles Warre Malet. Malet returned to England in 1798, bringing with him Wales's daughter, whom he married. He also brought Wales's drawings, which he showed to Thomas Daniell. Daniell had met the artist during his tour of western India in 1793 and he immediately recognised the potential of the images. In 1800 Malet published twelve of Wales's views of Bombay. Meanwhile, Thomas Daniell produced a number of aquatints, including an entire series of twenty-four devoted to the extraordinary system of rock-cut caves at Ellora based on Wales's sketches (see Chapter 3). Published in 1803, this series complemented Daniell's own volumes of *Oriental Scenery*. Many of the plates illustrate the richly decorated temples in great detail, but the book opens with a panoramic view showing some of the caves as small embellishments in a massive, idyllic landscape. Without the dedication of Malet and Daniell, James Wales's work might well have been lost to posterity.

Among the individual Europeans keen to commemorate their time in India by employing Indian and European artists, Warren Hastings and Robert Clive are probably the best known. Hastings, by virtue of his role as Governor-General at a crucial phase of East India Company expansion in India, is a pivotal figure in the history of British India. His patronage embraced a wide range of scholarship, art, literature and music, and it laid the foundations for the Asiatic Society of Bengal of 1784. He employed Indian musicians and was said to excel at the singing of 'Hindostannie airs'.[14] In the realm of the visual arts, he collected Indian paintings and was extremely generous to European painters: William Hodges travelled in India under his patronage and Zoffany received several lucrative commissions from him. Indeed, Hastings's perceived importance to the livelihoods of Europeans painters was such that, when Ozias Humphry arrived in Calcutta, he lamented for his prospects: 'The situation is not very favourable owing to the return of Warren Hastings who was a munificent patron.'[15] Humphry did not believe that Lord Cornwallis, Hastings's eventual successor, could match his predecessor and become a great a patron of the arts.[16]

We have seen how Robert Clive collected indigenous artefacts. Around 1771, Clive began to seek the advice of Benjamin West about buying Old Masters paintings for Claremont, his country residence at Esher in Surrey. When it came to contemporary art, Clive's tastes were relatively conservative and unadventurous: they rarely extended beyond the work of local portrait painters or landscapes by Claude-Joseph Vernet. However, Clive recognised that his erstwhile adviser also had artistic talents which could be harnessed to convey a particular message about Clive's time in India. Benjamin West was a versatile and influential painter of historical scenes, and would eventually succeed Sir Joshua Reynolds as President of the Royal Academy. Clive commissioned a series of vast canvases from West. Intended to depict the principal events of Clive's career in the subcontinent, these pictures were to be ranged around the walls of the dining room at Claremont. A surviving drawing shows two vast horizontal canvases on the east and west walls respectively, with a pair of vertical canvases over the fireplace. The canvases were to be displayed in plain gilt frames as part of an overall decorative scheme for the room, and interspersed with plasterwork 'enrichments' and roundels painted with elephants and camels, as well as Indians paying homage to a personification of Britannia.[17] Although the scheme was ultimately abandoned as a result of Clive's suicide in 1774, the Clive family and its Indian connections continued to

Figure 5.1
Indian artist,
'A View of the Ruins of Part of the Palace and Mosque at
Futtypoor Sicri (after William Hodges)', c. 1798–1804
(Add. Or. 1134)

play a part in presenting the country's engagement with India to audiences in Britain. Nearly half a century after Robert Clive had initiated contact with Benjamin West, the artist Joseph Farington recorded a visit to West's house in 1818:

> Before dinner Mr West took me into his great painting room & shewed me a large picture, ab[ou]t 18 feet wide of Lord Clive, accompanied by Gen. Carnack &c, receiving a paper of agreement from a Nabob. The picture He s[ai]d, is for the India House. The original picture of this subject He s[ai]d is to be completed and sent to Powis Castle near Welsh pool, & He is to paint another for Lord Clive, to be placed in his house in Shropshire.[18]

As the conversation with Farington suggests, Benjamin West painted several versions of this subject over the course of his long career. The depiction of Robert Clive receiving the grant of the *diwani* from the Mughal Emperor was a watershed moment in the history of the East India Company and the Clive family. Unsurprisingly, West's images would be closely connected with both. The painting seen by Farington was almost certainly the one exhibited at the Royal Academy the following May. As Farington recounts, it was subsequently sent to East India House in 1820, having been presented by Clive's son, the Earl of Powis. As we shall see, the decoration and adornment of the Company's headquarters with art and images played a major role in projecting and promoting its self-image as a powerful and influential institution.

However, it was not just the powerful nabobs or great figures in the Company's history who patronised the arts and encouraged the representation of India by European artists working there. William Hickey, an amateur draughtsman in his own right, declared himself to be 'as great an encourager of merits as my humble means would allow'. The arrival of 'the Messrs Daniell, uncle and nephew', in Bengal gave him an opportunity to make good on his assertion. By his own account, Hickey 'not only subscribed myself but procured many other names to a work they commenced upon of drawing and engraving in *aqua tinta*, twelve views of different parts of Calcutta'.[19] The example of George Chinnery, also detailed in Hickey's extensive memoirs, offers further evidence of the importance of local commissions and the circulation of images within the subcontinent. Chinnery was summoned from Madras to Calcutta in 1808 in order to paint a portrait of Sir Henry Russell, Chief Justice of the Supreme Court in Bengal. On this occasion, the commission was instigated by 'an elegant address in the Persian language' delivered by 'several of the principal natives of the settlement', which entreated Sir Henry to sit for a portrait to be exhibited in the Town Hall, a 'splendid building' then under construction.[20] Chinnery subsequently saw an opportunity to cash in on the commission and went about gathering subscriptions for an engraving based on the original oil painting. He needed 200 subscribers to cover his costs and was assured by William Hickey that 'there would be no difficulty in effecting that object, as I had the vanity to think I could command at least half the requisite number amongst my own immediate friends'. Hickey was as good as his word: 'I put about a paper headed with my own name for three copies, at three gold mohurs each copy, and soon got one hundred and seven subscribers.'[21] As we have seen, then, individuals, their tastes and interests played a major role in the representation of India by artists. However, just as the British economic and political engagement with India was brokered and deeply dependent on the East India Company, so the artistic encounter between India and Europe was heavily indebted to the Company and its patronage.

EXHIBITING EMPIRE: THE EAST INDIA COMPANY AND EAST INDIA HOUSE

On some levels, the East India Company could often appear to be uninterested in art. It was, after all, a business concern above all else, and the prospects of the Company supporting or even encouraging the arts often appeared remote. This was certainly the impression given to Thomas Hickey in Madras. He approached the authorities in 1804, hoping to be employed as the official history and portrait painter to the Company. If appointed, he reassured his readers, he would record the landscapes, monuments, races and customs of the country as well as 'British political and military transactions' there. Far from proposing a disinterested artistic endeavour, however, Hickey intended to emphasise the development of the British as 'imperial rulers of this eastern world'.[22] In this scenario, the Company was sure to play a starring role. But the merchants of Leadenhall Street declined the approach and flatly rejected the proposition: 'However much we wish the promotion of the useful and ingenious arts, the pursuits marked out by Mr Hickey must be left to the exertions of voluntary enterprise and the encouragement of private patronage.'[23]

The reality was more complex, however. Although the Company was rarely interested in art merely for the sake of decoration or display in its Indian territories, it employed Indian artists to help its officers make maps and prepare architectural drawings. For example, the Company paid an artist 100 rupees to accompany Francis Buchanan on his statistical survey of the Bengal Presidency in the early 1800s. And drawings for the buildings erected by the British were also often prepared by Indian draughtsmen.

The Company, then, *was* interested in visual representations. Indeed, it went to great lengths to ensure that the visual depictions of its territories and activities matched the confident self-image of a just and powerful ruler that it wanted to project to outsiders. Perhaps the most striking evidence of the Company's concern with collecting and displaying art, and using it to project an image of its commercial and territorial empire, was in its imposing headquarters on Leadenhall Street in the heart of the City of London. For visitors well connected or fortunate enough to gain entry to this impressive edifice, the interior was a rich mixture of images, sculptures and other objects that conveyed the Company's complex relationship with Asia. And the external decoration meant that even those who only walked past the building would have been left in no doubt as to the power and status of the institution.

As with many of its servants, the East India Company took a keen interest in representing India through three-dimensional objects. From its earliest days, the Company had maintained a storehouse or museum, composed of objects and specimens sent back by its servants working and travelling abroad.[24] The Company's enduring interest

Figure 5.2
George Lambert and Samuel Scott,
Fort William, Calcutta, c. 1731
(F45)

Figure 5.3
George Lambert and Samuel Scott,
Tellicherry Kerala, c. 1731 (F40)

in such scientific specimens and material culture as a way of presenting its involvement in India led to the formal establishment of a museum, located in East India House, in the early nineteenth century. In 1855 the Company's 'repository' was remodelled to reflect changing political imperatives about the value, utility and purpose of empire in the mid-nineteenth century. As a result, and although it still contained 'monumental and artistic records of the progress of the British Empire in the East', it also aimed 'to illustrate the productive resources of India and to give information about the life, manners, the arts and industry of its inhabitants'.[25] But, for most visitors, it was the decoration through images and sculptures that principally enlivened a visit to East India House. We have seen the example of John Dean, the shipwrecked mariner, whose portrait the Company commissioned to remind viewers of the importance of fortitude and endurance in the face of apparently insurmountable challenges. The other pictures on display in East India House were equally laden with associations and meaning. They reveal the complex connections between the Company and its growing empire in India, and the way in which they wanted to represent this back in Britain.

On a basic level, the paintings on display were potent visual reminders of the geographical sweep of the Company's activities. These images of the wider world underlined the international context and connections on which the Company's business success so depended. We have already explored the way in which George Lambert and Samuel Scott's series of paintings for the Directors' Court Room depicted key stations on the route to, and around the coast of, India (Figs 5.2 and 5.3; see Chapter 2). These works formed the visual centrepiece of the most important space in the entire building, the Directors' Court Room. But this was a recurring theme throughout East India House. For example, when he was recommissioned as a captain in the Madras Army in 1773, a grateful Francis Swain Ward presented ten landscape pictures to the Company, which subsequently hung in the meeting room of the Committee of Correspondence. In contrast to the maritime imagery and iconography of the Lambert and Scott series, the works by Ward represent some of the earliest depictions of Indian architecture and landscape by a British artist. Rest houses like the one depicted in A 'Choultry', or Travellers' Rest House, Srirangam, Madras were once ubiquitous features in southern India and were intended primarily for the benefit of travelling pilgrims (Fig. 5.4). The closely observed detail of the relatively modest building is complemented by the wider landscape context in which it has been set by Ward. Visitors to East India House would undoubtedly have been impressed by the window onto the Company's world given by these artists.

It was not just landscapes that adorned the walls of East India House. Portraits of various Asian rulers and emissaries presented in the hope of preferment, or as a reminder of the Company's reliance on them, were proof of the Company's links with Asia and its people. The three-quarter-length portrait of Nadir Shah, King of Persia, was a striking visual reminder of the complex network of local, indigenous rulers that the Company needed to engage with in order to maintain its position in India (Fig. 4.3). The King is depicted wearing a scarlet tunic with a sleeveless outer garment trimmed with fur. He wears a high cap (tahmazi) ornamented with a jewelled aigrette, and holds

a string of pearls in his right hand. The canvas was presented by Nicholas Vansittart to the Company in 1822, having been acquired in India by his father Henry Vansittart, the Governor of Fort William in the 1760s. The Court Minutes of 22 February 1822 recorded the offering and acceptance of the gift, as well as the subsequent order for the painting to be 'deposited in the Company's library'.[26]

Although the landscapes of India and portraits of local rulers might have presented novelty and a sense of exotic allure to visitors, the vast majority of East India House's walls and other display spaces were devoted to the rise of the Company in India and to the presentation and lionisation of its most successful servants. From the 1760s onwards, the internal decoration of the building reflected the pride that the Company took in its military and political successes. And individuals whose actions helped to propel the Company to its position of power in late eighteenth-century India were certain to find a place at the heart of the Company's headquarters.

Some of the earliest and most powerful visual representations of the Company's rise to prominence in India were found in the room where the leaders of the Company held their meetings: the Directors' Court Room. As the most important space in the building, where decisions were taken that affected the financial well-being of the Company as well as the lives and livelihoods of millions of people, the Directors' Court Room was suitably grand in its appearance. We get a sense of this from a watercolour by Thomas Shepherd in the middle of the nineteenth century (Fig. 5.5). Shepherd's image shows four of the six great 'settlement pictures' by Lambert and Scott. As we have seen, these depicted the Company's six main trading stations, as well as some of the vessels that visited them. Four of these pictures, showing Fort William and Tellicherry on the west wall (Figs 5.2 and 5.3), and St Helena and the Cape of Good Hope on the north wall (Figs 2.x and 2.x), are seen hanging above large framed mirrors. The two remaining pictures, depicting Fort St George and Bombay, are not visible (Figs 2.x and 2.x). The room was further enhanced by a large marble mantelpiece and accompanying overmantel, designed by the Dutch sculptor Michael Rysbrack and completed around the same time as the pictures. Two bearded figures support the mantelpiece, while a lion's pelt is draped between them. The overmantel provided an opportunity to present a symbolic sculptural depiction of the Company and its relationship with India and Asia more generally. It comprised an elaborate relief sculpture depicting Britannia receiving the riches of the East and symbolising the commerce of the Company. Britannia, shown seated under a rock beside the sea, looks eastwards as a personification of India approaches her and offers her a casket of jewels. Behind this, personifications of Asia and Africa lead a camel and a lion. To the left, two boys pour out treasures from a cornucopia. On the right, the Thames, depicted as a reed-crowned river-god, leans on the rudder of a ship. And in the background a man cording a bale and a fleet of sailing ships symbolise the labour, shipping and maritime activity on which the Company's success depended. This elaborate sculptural ensemble made the powerful point about the source of the East India Company's wealth and the key elements required to maintain its position.

While the decor of the Directors' Court Room represented the Company's success in its trading and commercial ventures, the decorative theme in the nearby Sale Room was quite different. Also known as the General Court Room, this was a large, cavernous space. Besides being the venue for general meetings of the Company's shareholders, or Proprietors, and auctions of goods, it became a hall of fame in which heroes of the Company were commemorated in marble (Figs 5.6 and 5.7). In 1760 the sculptor Peter Scheemakers was commissioned to produce three statues for niches in the room. The three figures to be celebrated in stone – Robert Clive, Major-General Stringer Lawrence and Sir George Pocock – had all played key roles in actions that saw the Company assert its supremacy over European and Indian rivals in the subcontinent. Having first sought their permission, the Proprietors ordered that 'their Portraits or Statues be taken in order to be placed in some conspicuous parts of this House, that their Eminent and Signal Services to this Company may be ever had in remembrance'.[27] Scheemakers completed his work in 1764, and the full-length figures dressed in suitably classical Roman attire were placed in niches, high above the large Sale Room, in which such daily activities as auctions of East India goods were conducted and meetings of the shareholders held. Gazing down from their niches, these figures exuded a classical air of detachment and order: Pocock was placed in the centre, flanked by Clive and Lawrence. Like Rysbrack's chimneypiece, these statues were also lit by natural light from the circular skylight above. To be carved in marble, rather than portrayed in the less expensive medium of oil paint, was a special honour and indicated the high esteem in which these men were held. Two further statues of military figures were later placed in other niches in the Sale Room. A commission to depict Sir Eyre Coote was executed by Thomas Banks in 1784, and ten years later John Bacon produced a likeness of Lord Cornwallis. The presence of these figures, and their representation in such severe classical format, would have confirmed the Company's evolution into an imperial organisation combining commercial, military and political functions.

Sculptural reminders of the Company's successes in India continued to be added to East India House in the nineteenth century. In 1820, two years after his death, the Company decided to pay a belated mark of respect to Warren Hastings by commissioning a statue of the former Governor-General from John Flaxman. Flaxman was one of the most sought-after sculptors of the day, and the price of the work reflected its creator's cultural cachet: the Company paid Flaxman £1,000. The finished work

Figure 5.5
Thomas Shepherd,
*The Directors' Court Room, East India House,
Leadenhall Street*, c. 1820 (WD2465)

Figure 5.6
Thomas Shepherd,
'The General Court Room, East India
House, Leadenhall Street, with a Meeting
of the Court of Proprietors in Progress',
c. 1820 (WD2466)

Figure 5.7
J. C. Stadler, after
Thomas Rowlandson and
Charles Augustus Pugin,
'India House, the Sale Room',
c. 1808–10 (P1571)

depicted Hastings standing in a niche, holding a rolled map of India and book of 'Hindu laws'. A couple of decades later, in 1841, Richard Wellesley was similarly honoured. On this occasion, Henry Weekes was charged with fulfilling the Company's resolution that, in recognition of

> the important services of the Most Noble the Marquis of Wellesley in establishing and consolidating the British Dominions in India upon a basis of Security which it never before possessed, a statue of His Lordship be placed in the General Court Room of this House as a public, conspicuous and permanent mark of the admiration and gratitude of the East India Company.[28]

Some figures were so important that they had multiple artworks commissioned in their honour. Stringer Lawrence was honoured again when his portrait by Joshua Reynolds was hung in a committee room, while Lord Cornwallis appeared in marble and oils. And in 1773, less than a decade after the unveiling of Scheemakers's statue, Robert Clive was represented in another artwork. On this occasion, Edward Penny was commissioned to depict Clive receiving a sum of money from the Nawab of Bengal (Fig. 5.8). In Penny's painting, Clive is shown receiving Mir Jafar's grant from his son Nawab Najim-ud-Daula, while pointing to a group of destitute soldiers. The subject of the painting was closely connected to its intended display space: the Military Fund Office in East India House. Edward Penny was a successful and prominent artist by the time he received this commission, having been appointed Professor of Painting at the newly established Royal Academy in 1768. After some haggling, the Company agreed to pay him 200 guineas for the work. Penny based the composition on his recent portrait of the Marquess of Granby relieving a sick soldier, a version of which was exhibited at the Society of Artists in 1765. However, despite the eminence of the artist and the nobility of the act, the critical response to the picture was decidedly mixed. When it was exhibited, the art critic of the *Morning Chronicle* noted somewhat caustically that, while 'want and disease in the faces of the invalids are likewise very powerfully marked', the figure of Lord Clive is 'neither expressive of humanity or dignity, at the same time 'tis reckoned an excellent likeness'.[29] Although Penny and Clive might have been perturbed by the criticism, it is unlikely to have worried the Company unduly. Indeed, the quality of the picture and the opinions of detractors were of secondary importance. With a parliamentary inquiry investigating Clive under way at the time, it is possible that the Company commissioned this painting and exhibited it publicly as a way of advertising its support for Clive and of bolstering his, and its own, reputation. The example of this painting underlines the fact that art played a number of roles in the context of the Company. Beyond simply providing decoration or aesthetic pleasure, it was often used to project a self-image. Nowhere could this be seen more clearly than in the external decoration of East India House.

It was not just on the interior walls of the Company's headquarters that the British relationship with India was depicted and displayed. East India House itself, and the various phases of its development, was a sophisticated record of the relationship

Figure 5.8
Edward Penny,
*Lord Clive Receiving from the Nawab of Bengal
the Grant of the Sum of Money which was Later
to Establish … 'Lord Clive's Fund'*, 1772–73 (F91)

Figure 5.9
George Vertue,
'The Old East India House, Leadenhall Street,
London', *c.* 1711 (WD1341)

Figure 5.10
Samuel Wale,
East India House, Leadenhall Street,
c. 1760
(WD2056)

between this private trading company and the subcontinent. Over the course of its lifetime, the architecture of the East India Company's headquarters provided physical and visual parallels to its trading and political power: it went from small beginnings to grand opulence and then almost complete erasure. The Company's earliest home was the front room of its first governor, Thomas Smythe, at his house in Philpot Lane. It met there for some twenty years; two centuries later East India House stood on a much larger site, covering one and a half acres, and employed hundreds of clerks.

Like most of the chartered companies that brokered Britain's relationship with the rest of the world, the East India Company's premises were located at the heart of the City of London. During the early years of its fragile existence, the Company leased several modest sites in the City that acted in turn as the headquarters for the fledgling trading corporation. In 1647 the Company established a permanent home in Leadenhall Street when a lease was taken out on a building owned by Lord Craven. 'Craven House', as it was originally known, stood beside the busy Leadenhall Market, at the junction of Lime Street and Leadenhall Street. The building was convenient for both stockholders and officials, being close to the capital's financial institutions, the river Thames and the Company's several warehouses. The Company eventually purchased the site in 1710, and its headquarters remained at this location until the Company's demise in the mid-nineteenth century.

The old East India House, depicted by George Vertue in a drawing of 1711 (Fig. 5.9), was progressively reconstructed and enlarged during the eighteenth century, a process which reflected the progress of the Company's commercial and political fortunes. The original, cramped wooden house had become rather dilapidated by the 1720s and, between 1726 and 1729, it was replaced by a much grander building designed by the architect Theodore Jacobsen (Fig. 5.10). Although elements of the design drew inspiration from recent developments in British and European architecture, such as Palladianism and Neoclassicism, it was still a relatively simple, four-storey stone structure. Jacobsen's building extended far back from the street and had large rooms for the directors and spacious offices for the clerks. There was also a hall, a garden and a courtyard for receptions. In appearance, the architecture was solid and suitably reassuring, displaying British values of common sense and stability, precisely the characteristics required to inspire confidence in shareholders subscribing to risky long-distance trading ventures.

But the Company's success soon outgrew this modest structure. Less than half a century after Jacobsen completed his work, there were calls for another upgrade. Some people felt that the organisation's activities, ambitions and responsibilities – particularly after the acquisition of the *diwani* in 1765 – warranted a further expansion and redevelopment of its main administrative building in London. In 1773, for example, James Northouck remarked that 'the appearance of the building is nowise suited to the opulence of the Company, whose servants exercise sovereign authority in their Indian territories and live there in a princely state'.[30] And the opinions of Sir John Fielding, offered in 1776, demonstrate the close connection that was drawn by contemporaries between business success and architectural grandeur:

> East India House (Leadenhall Street) is a plain Doric structure, on a rustic base, in which there is not much to praise or much to censure, though deemed by persons of perhaps over-nice taste inadequate to the Wealth, Consequence and Power of the Proprietors. It must be confessed that the House is too small in front, when we consider the importance of the … business carried on there.[31]

However, despite the strictures of Northouck, Fielding and others, it would be another twenty years before further major refurbishments were undertaken at East India House.

When this renovation work eventually took place, between 1796 and 1799, it similarly reflected the Company's status and pretensions (Fig. 5.11). Passers-by could not fail to admire the size and scale of the directors' ambitions. This was development on a grand scale, with the purchase of a number of nearby houses and taverns in Lime Street and Leadenhall Street permitting the expansion of the site. The work was supervised by Richard Jupp, the Company surveyor, who died in April 1799, and his successor, Henry Holland. Jupp had been surveyor to the East India Company since 1768. As part of this role, he had designed several London warehouses, starting with the Old Bengal Warehouse on New Street (1769–71) with extensions towards Cutler Street and Middlesex Street in the 1790s. But the task at Leadenhall Street was of an entirely different order of magnitude. For starters, there were internal readjustments: a new central corridor was added as well as a more spacious Sale Room. But it was the façade, fronting onto Leadenhall Street, that really captured the spirit of the Company at the apogee of its power and connected this London street with a distant continent. The new façade left onlookers in little doubt as to the success and wealth of the Company, or of its importance to the British economy and to British prestige more generally. Measuring 190 feet in length and 60 feet in height, it was composed of six Ionic pillars surmounted by a richly decorated pediment and tympanum. The sculptural programme in the tympanum (the triangular space enclosed by the pediment) was the work of John Bacon. Bacon had risen to prominence in the London art world and was perhaps best known for his statue of Admiral George Rodney which stood in Spanish Town, Jamaica. This had led to other commissions, most notably for the huge figures of 'Fame' and the 'Genius of England', together with George III and the River Thames, that embellished Somerset House on the Strand. And Bacon had worked for the East India Company before, when the directors commissioned a marble portrait statue of Lord Cornwallis. But Bacon's work on the façade of the Company's headquarters was a much more public statement of status and authority. High above the London streetscape, it depicted George III in Roman costume shielding personifications of Britannia and Asia. To the King's right, 'Commerce' was represented by 'Mercury attended by navigation, triton, horse, [and] elephant, with the Ganges', while to his left sat 'order attended by religion, industry and integrity, the City Barge, and the Thames'.[32] On top of the pediment itself stood Britannia with a lion, holding a spear and bearing a cap of Liberty in her left hand. On either side were two figures: Europe on a horse and Asia on a camel. The entire ensemble was a deeply symbolic work, encapsulating the way in which the East India Company wanted passers-by to understand its relationship with India. By combining commerce and trade, the foundations of the Company's wealth and power, with abstract ideas like liberty, religion and industry, Bacon's work emphasised 'what Britain can bring to the East in exchange for the bounty of India'.[33]

The presence of George III reminded everybody, including the Company itself, that the Company's charter and its role in India were increasingly circumscribed by parliamentary legislation. Bacon's scheme was prophetic. As the eighteenth century gave way to the nineteenth, the British state, symbolised here by the King, would become increasingly involved in regulating the Company and administering its responsibilities in India. Barely fifty years after Bacon completed his work, it would vanish, along with East India House itself. The grand edifice on Leadenhall Street, a potent symbol of the Company's wealth, power and status for so long, disappeared only a few years after 1858, when the East India Company went out of business. However, in a move laden with heavy symbolism, the art that adorned the walls of East India House was transplanted to the newly formed India Office in Whitehall. The end of the Company marked the start of another chapter in the history of the British engagement with India.

Figure 5.11
Thomas Malton,
'The East India Company's Headquarters in
Leadenhall Street, as rebuilt by Richard Jupp
and Henry Holland in 1796–1799', 1800
(WD2460)

CHAPTER 6

Conclusion: The end of the Company

At the same time as Richard Jupp was refurbishing East India House in London, the Company's headquarters in India were also undergoing a transformation. The building of a new Government House in Calcutta was begun in February 1799 and completed four years later. Richard Wellesley, the Governor-General behind this hugely costly scheme, would undoubtedly have agreed with those who expected the Company's physical buildings to reflect its wealth and political importance. This new Government House, the seat of Company power in Bengal, was intended to advertise the significance and status of this institution. As he told Lord Valentia, Wellesley wanted India 'to be ruled from a palace, not a counting house; with the ideas of a Prince, not those of a retail dealer in muslins and indigos'.[1]

According to William Hickey, Wellesley 'determined upon building a palace suitable to his magnificent ideas, and such a one as would be proper for the residence of the British Governor General of India':

> This he immediately caused to be commenced, partly upon the site of the old Government House, but taking in the Council House and about sixteen other handsome private mansions, many of them not having been erected above five years, the whole of which were pulled down, the ground upon which they had stood being cleared away to create a superb open square area, in the middle of which his meditated palace was to stand.[2]

Wellesley plumped for a neoclassical design by Charles Wyatt, an officer in the Bengal Engineers (and a member of the famous family of architects), to fill the vast site on Esplanade Row (Figs 6.1 and 6.2). Wyatt's design was not entirely original: just as Indian designs influenced Company servants returning to Britain, so European architectural styles inspired Wyatt and Wellesley in Calcutta. In fact, the plan for the new Government House was modelled on that of Kedleston Hall in Derbyshire, so that Wellesley could truly be said to be transplanting a grand English country house to the heart of the Company's Raj in India. A grand portico of Ionic columns and a flight of steps formed the main entrance to the building. And the four magnificent gateways on the perimeter of the garden were partly based on Robert Adam's design for the gateway to Syon House near London. As with East India House in Leadenhall Street, the interior decoration projected wealth, power and authority. The magnificent state dining room, the Marble Hall, incorporated busts of the twelve Caesars ranged along its walls as well as an elaborate ceiling painting. The Throne Room housed the throne of Tipu Sultan, recently captured from his capital, Seringapatam, in 1799. The symbolism of incorporating the regal accoutrements of an Indian ruler into the regalia of the Company's headquarters in the subcontinent made a powerful statement.

In his characteristically abrasive way, Wellesley pushed ahead with the expensive programme without recourse to, or the sanction of, the directors of the Company in London, his notional superiors. It was only later, in a retrospective and belated attempt to persuade the Company's directors of the importance of the scheme, that Wellesley sent a letter of explanation and drawings by James Best to Leadenhall Street in order

Detail of Figure 6.6
William Roberts and Lowes Dickinson, after Charles D'Oyly, 'Town and Port of Calcutta', in Charles D'Oyly, *Views of Calcutta and its Environs,* 1848 (X 666)

Figure 6.1
James Moffat,
New Government House, c. 1803–4
(WD 476)

Figure 6.2
Indian artist,
*View of the North Front of Government House
with the Marquess of Hastings Leaving It, c.* 1817
(Add. Or. 3309)

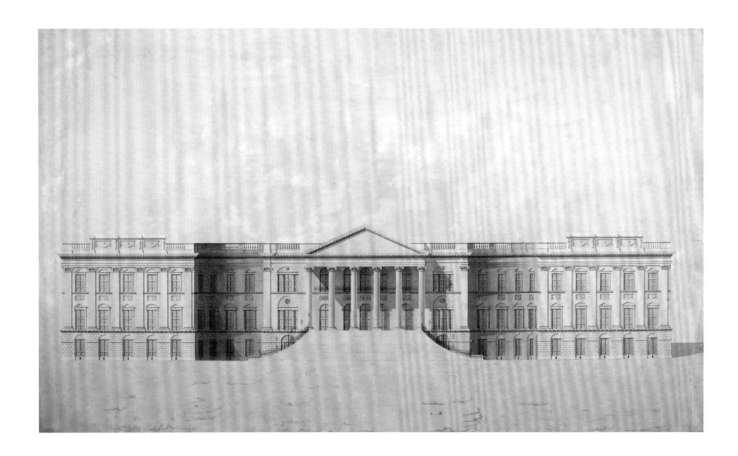

to illustrate the impressive structure that he was building on their behalf in Calcutta (Figs 6.3 and 6.4).

Wellesley's plans for Government House represented more than simply a building project. The new edifice on Esplanade Row identified the Company as a great political and imperial power in addition to its commercial success. This corresponded to wider changes affecting the Company and the British engagement with the subcontinent more generally. The reasons for this development are complex – located in a combination of domestic British politics, local Indian politics and broader global developments – and are still debated by historians. But the general trend is clear. In many ways, then, Wellesley's scheme symbolised the evolution of the Company. Thomas Pownall expressed what many others thought about the growth of this commercial company in the third quarter of the eighteenth century: 'The merchant is become the sovereign ... a trading company have in their hands the exercise of a sovereignty.'[3] Robert Clive gave even more detail when he appeared before the House of Commons in 1769. He contrasted the current position of the Company with that of 1744, when he had first stepped ashore at Madras: 'I was in India when the Company was established for the

Figure 6.3
James Best,
Elevation of the North West front of the New Government House, c. 1803
(WD1319)

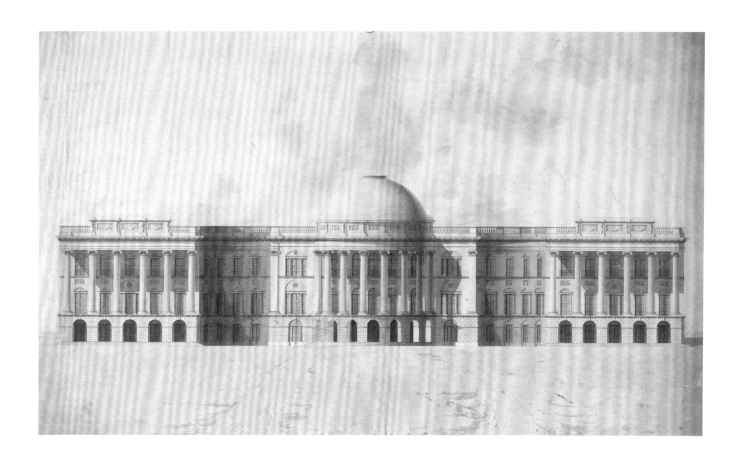

Figure 6.4
James Best,
*Elevation of the South East front of
the New Government House, c.* 1803
(WD1320)

purposes of trade only, when their fortifications scarce deserved that name, when their possessions were within very narrow bounds.' Now, however, the Company had changed into something entirely more powerful:

> The East India Company are at this time sovereigns of a rich, populous, fruitful country in extent beyond France and Spain united; they are in possession of the labour, industry, and manufactures of twenty million of subjects; they are in actual receipt of between five and six millions a year. They have an army of fifty thousand men. The revenues of Bengal are little short of four million sterling a year. Out of this revenue the East India Company, clear of all expenses receives £1,600,000 a year.[4]

By the end of the century, the Company had undoubtedly become more than a mere merchant, as represented most forcefully in the new Government House envisaged by Wellesley. It had become the sovereign power of a vast sweep of Indian territory and, in the first half of the nineteenth century, it would be confronted with all of the

Figure 6.5
Thomas Prinsep,
The Steamer Hooghley on the River Ganges, 1828
(WD4194)

problems associated with territorial and political power. The Company's rise to power and prominence, and the heightened importance of India to both the British economy and the British sense of global prestige, meant that the Company came under heightened scrutiny in London and increasing pressure in India.

And there were other changes afoot too. Technology would play a major role in the development of British power in India, particularly as the nineteenth century progressed. The early signs of this are evident in a watercolour by Thomas Prinsep showing a new steam vessel on the river Ganges (Fig. 6.5). Prinsep learned drawing from T. H. Fielding at the East India Company Military Seminary at Addiscombe in Surrey. He joined the Bengal Engineers in 1818 and was subsequently employed in cutting a series of canals, before being appointed Superintendent of Canals in 1826. This image is taken from an album of thirteen watercolours recording the memorable voyage undertaken by Prinsep in 1828. The Governor-General at the time, Lord William Bentinck, wanted to know whether steam navigation was practicable on the Ganges, which would significantly reduce the time spent travelling upcountry. Captain Johnson commanded the *Hooghley*, a Calcutta-built wooden paddle-steamer, with a twenty-five-horsepower steam engine imported from Britain. The trip was a success: the round voyage of 1,000 miles to Allahabad was cut to just six weeks, down from the three months it normally took just to get to Allahabad. Commenting on his brother's work, William Prinsep did not neglect the artistic effect of such work:

> Tom made a series of the most beautiful drawings of the Ganges during the voyage portraying the peculiar colour of the water during the season and the lovely effects of blues over the picturesque fleets of native boats making their slow way against the fierce current.[5]

However, this image also marks a new phase in the development of transport and communications in British India. The same impression is conveyed in a view of Calcutta by Charles D'Oyly, and subsequently reproduced as a hand-coloured lithograph for wider dissemination in his *Views of Calcutta and its Environs* published in 1848 (Fig. 6.6). D'Oyly depicts the *maidan*, the park-like setting flanking the water's edge just beyond Fort William, the nucleus of the Company's military power in the city. We get a sense of the way travel had changed by this time. European civilians stroll around as clippers, a steamship and a variety of local boats crowd the water's edge. John Bellew was struck with wonder in describing the scene that greeted him in the early 1840s:

OVERLEAF
Figure 6.6
William Roberts and Lowes Dickinson,
after Charles D'Oyly, 'Town and Port of Calcutta', in Charles
D'Oyly, *Views of Calcutta and its Environs*, 1848 (X 666)

I have seen few sights in my wanderings more beautiful and imposing than the approach to this Petersburgh of the East, this magnificent capital of our eastern empire. ... Numerous boats glide up and down the river. ... All, in fact, bespoke the close vicinity of a great capital.[6]

Developments in travel and communications were matched by a new questioning of the ultimate purpose and value of Britain's imperial possessions. For example, Claudius Buchanan, a Company chaplain and Professor of Greek and Latin at the college at Fort William, identified the wider spiritual mission that he believed went hand in hand with the expansion of the British Empire, the defeat of Revolutionary and Napoleonic France, and the growth of British India:

Our extensive territorial acquisitions within the last few years, our recent triumph over our only formidable foe; and the avowed consequence of India in relation to the existing state of Europe; and that unexampled and systematic prosperity of Indian administrations, which has now consolidated the British dominion in this country – every character of our situation seems to mark the present æra, as that intended by Providence, for our taking into consideration the moral and religious state of our subjects in the East; and for Britain's bringing up her long arrear of duty, and settling her account honourably with her Indian Empire.[7]

The feeling that God had entrusted Britain with its imperial responsibilities led to further developments that would translate, for example, into the British drive to eliminate local and, to British eyes, detestable practices such as suttee (or sati), whereby widows threw themselves onto their husband's funeral pyres. But it also led to tension and suspicion in India as the old practices of the Company came under greater scrutiny.

Political, technological and social changes in the early nineteenth century transformed Britain's relationship with India. Increasingly embattled at home, the East India Company's rule was also under threat in India itself. The outbreak of mutiny and rebellion across northern India in 1857 was the spark that heralded the end of the Company and the beginnings of the formal British Raj. The crisis erupted at Meerut on 9 and 10 May when the sepoys stationed there killed their European officers and set off on the road to Delhi, forty miles to the south-west. Popular rebellion spread rapidly as the Company's Bengal army mutinied, or attempted to mutiny, practically everywhere from the borders of Bengal to the gates of Lahore. Although the uprising was eventually suppressed, it changed things irrevocably. As early as 1857, civil officers in the North-Western Provinces claimed that the uprising was due to insensitivity among the British military establishment for Hindu 'caste prejudices'. The military responded by saying that heavy tax burdens, and a high-handed approach to dealing with local rulers, who were sidelined and stripped of their authority, were really to blame. These factors were compounded, they argued, by the ill-advised annexations of several local states as a consequence of Lord Dalhousie's 'Doctrine of Lapse', a controversial policy which gave the British Governor-General the right to annex an Indian state or province if the incumbent ruler died without a male heir or was deemed incompetent. Whatever the causes of the uprising – and it has long been a topic of controversy and debate among historians – it was clear that the East India Company could no longer govern India effectively. The passing of an Act of Parliament in Westminster transferred the Company's assets and responsibilities to the British government in Whitehall and brought an end to this particular chapter of the relationship between India and Britain.

Although 1858 signalled the end of the East India Company, its impact on the visual representation of India was crucial, far reaching and long lasting. *Picturing India* has demonstrated the enduring importance of visual representations in brokering that relationship between Britain and India. Images of Indian people and places had long helped to mediate and define Britain's engagement with the subcontinent. The portraits and landscapes produced by artists like Johan Zoffany, William Hodges, Thomas Daniell and others provide a powerful and evocative insight into the ways in which they and their patrons envisaged India.

ENDNOTES

1 William Hodges, *Travels in India during the Years 1780, 1781, 1782, & 1783* (London: printed for the author, sold by J. Edwards, 1793), p. iii.
2 'The East India House', *Leisure Hour*, 5 September 1861, p. 567.
3 Hodges, *Travels in India*, p. iii.
4 P. J. Marshall, 'Taming the Exotic: The British and India in the Seventeenth and Eighteenth Centuries', in G. S. Rousseau and Roy Porter (eds), *Exoticism in the Enlightenment* (Manchester: Manchester University Press, 1990), pp. 46–65, p. 46.
5 James Rennell, *Memoir of a Map of Hindoostan; or The Mogul Empire* (London: James Rennell, 1788), p. v.
6 Hodges, *Travels in India*, pp. 31–2.
7 Royal Academy of Arts, London, Ozias Humphry papers (RAA), HU/3/132, Ozias Humphry to Philip Yonge, 14 March 1787.
8 Hodges, *Travels in India*, p. 2
9 British Library, Add. MS 29142, pp. 276–7, John Macpherson to Warren Hastings, 31 December 1778.
10 Hodges, *Travels in India*, p. 10.
11 Hodges, *Travels in India*, p. 27.
12 Quoted in Hermione de Almeida and George H. Gilpin, *Indian Renaissance: British Romantic Art and the Prospect of India* (Aldershot: Ashgate, 2005), p. 41.
13 Quoted in Mildred Archer and R. Lightbown, *India Observed: India as Viewed by British Artists, 1760–1860* (London: Victoria and Albert Museum, 1982), pp. 86–7.
14 Paul Sandby to James Gandon [1783], quoted in De Almeida and Gilpin, *Indian Renaissance*, p. 73.
15 RAA, HU/3/55, Ozias Humphry to Rev. William Humphry, 3 April 1786.
16 Thomas Daniell and William Daniell, *A Picturesque Voyage to India by the Way of China* (London: Longman, 1810), pp. i–ii.
17 Quoted in Thomas Sutton, *The Daniells: Artists and Travellers* (London: Bodley Head, 1954), p. 92.
18 RAA, HU/4/24–5, Claude Martin to Ozias Humphry, 11 March 1789.
19 Quoted in Jeremiah P. Losty, *Calcutta: City of Palaces. A Survey of the City in the Days of the East India Company, 1690–1858* (London: British Library, 1990), p. 48.
20 Thomas Twining, *Travels in India a Hundred Years Ago* (London: Osgood, McIlvaine and Co., 1893), pp. 74–5.
21 William Hickey, *Memoirs of William Hickey*, edited by Alfred Spencer, 4 vols (London: Hurst and Blackett, 1948), vol. 3, p. 342.
22 Quoted in De Almeida and Gilpin, *Indian Renaissance*, p. 41.
23 Hodges, *Travels in India*, pp. iv, vi.
24 Jemima Kindersley, *Letters from the Island of Teneriffe, Brazil, the Cape of Good Hope, and the East Indies* (London: J. Nourse, 1777), pp. 74–5.
25 RAA, HU/1/98, C. Imhof [*sic*] to Ozias Humphry, 27 December 1770.
26 Quoted in Mildred Archer, *India and British Portraiture: 1770–1825* (London: Sotheby's, 1979), p. 121.
27 RAA, HU/2/130, Gavin Hamilton to Ozias Humphry, 12 December 1792.
28 RAA, HU/4/88–9, William Baillie to Ozias Humphry, 23 November 1793.
29 Rennell, *Memoir of a Map of Hindoostan*, p. iii.
30 University of Southampton, Hartley Library Special Collections, Broadlands Papers, BR 11/14/8, Benjamin Mee to Viscount Palmerston, 8 December 1789.
31 Quoted in Bernard Smith, *European Vision and the South Pacific* (New Haven and London: Yale University Press, 1985), p. 203.
32 RAA, HU/4/18, Gavin Hamilton to Ozias Humphry, 15 February 1789.
33 Quoted in Richard Altick, *The Shows of London* (Cambridge, MA: Harvard University Press, 1978), p. 135.

CHAPTER 2

1 'Edmund Burke on the Impeachment of Warren Hastings, 15–19 February 1788', in Barbara Harlow and Mia Carter (eds), *Archives of Empire*, vol. 1: *From the East India Company to the Suez Canal* (Durham, NC, and London: Duke University Press, 2003), pp. 143–55, p. 147.
2 'Account of the Battle of Plassey, Gained by the Brave Col. Clive', *London Magazine; or, Gentleman's Monthly Intelligencer* (January 1760), pp. 7–8, p. 8.
3 Quoted in Mildred Archer, 'The East India Company and British Art', *Apollo* 82 (1965), pp. 401–9, p. 406.
4 Quoted in K. N. Chaudhuri, *The Trading World of Asia and the English East India Company* (Cambridge: Cambridge University Press, 1978), p. 454.
5 Warren Hastings to Court of Directors, 11 November 1773, in G. R. Gleig, *Memoirs of the Life of the Right Hon. Warren Hastings, first Governor-General of Bengal*, 3 vols (London: Richard Bentley, 1843), vol. 1, p. 368.
6 [H. T. Colebrooke and A. Lambert], *Remarks on the Present State of the Husbandry and Commerce of Bengal* (Calcutta, 1795), pp. 64–5, quoted in P. J. Marshall, 'Taming the Exotic: The British and India in the Seventeenth and Eighteenth Centuries', in G. S. Rousseau and Roy Porter (eds), *Exoticism in the Enlightenment* (Manchester: Manchester University Press, 1990), pp. 46–65, p. 56.
7 *European Magazine and London Review* 23 (June 1793), p. 403.
8 Quoted in P. J. Marshall and Glyndwr Williams, *The Great Map of Mankind: British Perceptions of the World in the Age of Enlightenment* (Cambridge, MA: Harvard University Press, 1982), p. 155.
9 Governor-General in Council, Fort William, to the Honourable Court of Directors, 9 July 1800, in *The Despatches, Minutes, and Correspondence of the Marquess Wellesley*, ed. Robert Montgomery Martin, 5 vols (London: William H. Allen, 1836), vol. 2, pp. 320, 312.
10 William H. Carey, *The Good Old Days of Honourable John Company* (1882) (Calcutta: Quins Book Co., 1964), p. 77.
11 Royal Academy of Arts, London, Ozias Humphry papers (RAA), HU/5/88, William Sydenham to Ozias Humphry, 10 October 1800.
12 RAA, HU/2/130, Gavin Hamilton to Ozias Humphry, 12 December 1792.
13 RAA, HU/3/49–50, Ozias Humphry to Mary Boydell, 29 December 1785.
14 See, for example, British Library (BL), India Office Records (IOR), E/3/90, pp. 89–98, 1 August 1683.
15 BL, IOR, G/32/165, pp. 2, 4, Robert Brooke, 'Account of St Helena with Various Observations Annexed' [1792].
16 BL, IOR, H/88, p. 392, Dissent of Jacob Bosanquet to the plan proposed by Thomas Grenville, 15 October 1806.
17 Thomas Daniell and William Daniell, 'Western Entrance of Fort St George', *Oriental Scenery*, II, plate 12.
18 Thomas Daniell and William Daniell, 'South East View of Fort St George, Madras', *Oriental Scenery*, II, plate 7.
19 William Hodges, *Travels in India during the Years 1780, 1781, 1782, & 1783* (London: printed for the author, sold by J. Edwards, 1793), pp. 1–2.
20 James Main, 'Reminiscences of a Voyage to and from China', Paxton's *Horticultural Register and General Magazine* 5 (1836), pp. 98–9, quoted in Georgina Green, *Sir Charles Raymond of Valentines and the East India Company* (London: Hainault Press, 2015), p. 10.
21 Thomas Daniell and William Daniell, 'South East View of Fort St George, Madras', *Oriental Scenery*, II, plate 7.
22 Anon., *A Description of the Port and Island of Bombay: And an Historical Account of the Transactions between the English and Portugueze concerning it, from the Year 1661 to the Present Time* (London: s.n., 1724), p. 4, quoted in Timothy Davies, 'English Private Trade on the West Coast of India, c. 1680–c. 1740', *Itinerario* 38 (2014), pp. 51–73, p. 63.
23 Hodges, *Travels in India*, pp. 14–16.
24 Quoted in P. J. Marshall, *Bengal: The British Bridgehead: Eastern India, 1740–1828* (Cambridge: Cambridge University Press, 1988), p. 160.
25 Quoted in Jeremiah P. Losty, *Calcutta: City of Palaces. A Survey of the City in the Days of the East India Company, 1690–1858* (London: British Library, 1990), pp. 44, 36.
26 Eliza Fay to 'My Dear Friends', 22 May 1780, in Eliza Fay, *Original Letters from India* (Calcutta: s.n., 1817), pp. 238, 239, 239–40.
27 Quoted in Mildred Archer, *Early Views of India: The Picturesque Journeys of Thomas and William Daniell, 1786–1794* (London: Thames and Hudson, 1980), p. 14.
28 Hodges, *Travels in India*, p. 14.

CHAPTER 3

1 William Hodges, *Travels in India during the Years 1780, 1781, 1782, & 1783* (London: printed for the author, sold by J. Edwards, 1793), pp. 31–2.
2 Hodges, *Travels in India*, pp. 25–6.
3 University of Southampton, Hartley Library Special Collections, Broadlands Papers, BR 11/11/4, Benjamin Mee to Viscount Palmerston, 9 January 1786.
4 Quoted in Romita Ray, *Under the Banyan Tree: Relocating the Picturesque in British India* (New Haven and London: Yale University Press, 2013), p. 129.
5 William Hickey, *Memoirs of William Hickey*, edited by Alfred Spencer, 4 vols (London: Hurst and Blackett, 1948), vol. 2, p. 120.
6 Thomas Twining, *Travels in India a Hundred Years Ago* (London: Osgood, McIlvaine and Co., 1893), p. 73.
7 Quoted in Ray, *Under the Banyan Tree*, p. 129.
8 George [Annesley], Viscount Valentia, *Voyages and Travels to India, Ceylon, the Red Sea, Abyssinia, and Egypt, in the Years 1802, 1803, 1804, 1805, and 1806*, 4 vols (London: F., C., and J. Rivington, 1811), vol. 1, p. 40.
9 Quoted in Jeremiah P. Losty, *Calcutta: City of Palaces. A Survey of the City in the Days of the East India Company, 1690–1858* (London: British Library, 1990), p. 80.
10 Quoted in Ray, *Under the Banyan Tree*, pp. 128–9.
11 Hickey, *Memoirs of William Hickey*, vol. 4, p. 237.
12 'An Account of the Caves of Cannara, Ambala, and Elephanta, … in a letter from Hector Macneil', *Archaeologia* 8 (1788), p. 260, quoted in P. J. Marshall, 'Taming the Exotic: The British and India in the Seventeenth and Eighteenth Centuries', in G. S. Rousseau and Roy Porter (eds), *Exoticism in the Enlightenment* (Manchester: Manchester University Press, 1990), pp. 46–65, p. 62.
13 Quoted in Partha Mitter, *Much Maligned Monsters: A History of European Reactions to Indian Art* (Oxford: Clarendon Press, 1977), p. 172.
14 Quoted in Hermione de Almeida and George H. Gilpin, *Indian Renaissance: British Romantic Art and the Prospect of India* (Aldershot: Ashgate, 2005), p. 126.
15 Charles Malet, 'Description of the Caves or Excavations on the Mountain … Eastward of the Town of Ellora', *Asiatick Researches* 6 (1801), pp. 382–423, p. 386.
16 British Library, India Office Library, MSS Eur. D. 1160/1, William Prinsep, 'The Memoirs of William Prinsep', vol. 2, p. 260, quoted in Malcolm Allbrook, *Henry Prinsep's Empire: Framing a Distant Colony*

(Canberra: Australian National University Press, 2014), p. 52.

17 James Baillie Fraser, *Journal of a Tour through part of the Snowy Range of the Himala Mountains* (London: Rodwell and Martin, 1820), p. 478.

18 Samuel Turner, *An Account of an Embassy to the Court of the Teshoo Lama in Tibet* (London: s.n., 1800), p. 139.

19 Quoted in Mildred Archer, *Early Views of India: The Picturesque Journeys of Thomas and William Daniell, 1786–1794* (London: Thames and Hudson, 1980), p. 49.

20 Hodges, *Travels in India*, p. 94.

21 Valentia, *Voyages and Travels to India, Ceylon, the Red Sea, Abyssinia, and Egypt*, vol. 1, pp. 292–3.

22 Quoted in Archer, *Early Views of India*, fig. 57.

23 Quoted in Ray, *Under the Banyan Tree*, pp. 203–4.

24 François Bernier, *Travels in the Mogol Empire, A.D. 1656–1668*, translated by Irving Brock and revised by Archibald Constable (London: Archibald Constable, 1891), p. 5.

25 Twining, *Travels in India a Hundred Years Ago*, p. 194.

26 Thomas Daniell and William Daniell, *Views of the Taje Mahal at the City of Agra in Hindoostan Taken in 1789* (London: s.n.,1801), p. 3.

27 State Library of Western Australia, Acc. 499A, Henry C. Prinsep, 'Diaries, 1866–1922', 28 May 1870, quoted in Allbrook, *Henry Prinsep's Empire*, p. 128.

28 Hodges, *Travels in India*, p. 124.

29 Archer, *Early Views of India*, p. 43.

30 Daniell and Daniell, *Views of the Taje Mahel*, pp. 5–6.

31 Bernier, *Travels in the Mogol Empire*, p. 334.

32 William Sproston Caine, *Picturesque India: A Handbook for European Travellers* (London: George Routledge and Son, 1891), p. 301.

33 Hodges, *Travels in India*, p. 47.

34 Caine, *Picturesque India*, p. 302.

35 Quoted in Ray 1, *Under the Banyan Tree*, p. 31.

36 *The Hindoos* (1834), vol. 1, p. 213, quoted in W. G. Archer, 'Benares through the Eyes of British Artists', *Apollo* 92 (1970), pp. 96–103, pp. 96–8.

37 Hodges, *Travels in India*, pp. 47, 59.

38 Hodges, *Travels in India*, pp. 60–1.

39 Hodges, *Travels in India*, p. 52.

40 Quoted in Pratapaditya Pal and Vidya Dehejia, *From Merchants to Emperors: British Artists and India, 1757–1930* (Ithaca and London: Cornell University Press, 1986), pp. 98–9.

41 Quoted in Pal and Dehejia, *From Merchants to Emperor*, p. 99.

42 Quoted in C. A. Bayly (ed.), *Raj: The British and India* (London: National Portrait Gallery, 1990), pp. 210–11.

43 Royal Academy of Arts, London, Ozias Humphry papers (RAA), HU/4/112–17, William Baillie to Ozias Humphry, 4 October–7 November 1795.

CHAPTER 4

1 Royal Academy of Arts, London, Ozias Humphry papers (RAA), HU/4/112–17, William Baillie to Ozias Humphry, 4 October–7 November 1795.

2 William Hickey, *Memoirs of William Hickey*, edited by Alfred Spencer, 4 vols (London: Hurst and Blackett, 1948), vol. 4, pp. 232, 249, 250.

3 Tillman W. Nechtman, 'Mr Hickey's Pictures: Britons and their Collectibles in Late Eighteenth-Century India', in Barry Crosbie and Mark Hampton (eds), *The Cultural Construction of the British World* (Manchester: Manchester University Press, 2015), pp. 180–97, p. 182.

4 RAA, HU/3/92, Edward Brown to Ozias Humphry, December 1785.

5 Sir John Macpherson to Asaf-ud-Daula, quoted in Mildred Archer, *India and British Portraiture, 1770–1825* (London: Sotheby's, 1979), p. 389.

6 Hickey, *Memoirs of William Hickey*, vol. 2, p. 157.

7 RAA, HU/4/13, Thomas Daniell to Ozias Humphry, 7 November 1788.

8 Quoted in George C. Williamson, *Life and Works of Ozias Humphry, R.A.* (London: John Lane, 1918), p. 144.

9 RAA, HU/3/99, D. MacKinnon to Ozias Humphry, 21 January 1786.

10 Quoted in Archer, *India and British Portraiture*, p. 133.

11 The painting, entitled *Colonel Antoine Polier, Claude Martin and John Wombwell with the Artist*, is in the collection of the Victoria Memorial Hall, Kolkata.

12 The painting is now in the Tate Collection (T06856).

13 *Madras Courier*, 26 November 1806, quoted in Archer, *India and British Portraiture*, p. 363.

14 Quoted in Archer, *India and British Portraiture*, p. 364.

15 The ship's captain, Henry Wilson, recorded in his log that 'suddenly the people in the boats discharged a flight of arrows at us'. See the logbook of the *Antelope*, 1 April 1783, BL OIOC, L/Mar/B/570A.

16 *Calcutta Gazette*, 18 October 1792, quoted in Archer, *India and British Portraiture*, pp. 256–7.

17 On his facility for painting shipping, see RAA, HU/4/88–89, William Baillie to Ozias Humphry, 23 November 1793.

18 Quoted in Mildred Archer and R. Lightbown, *India Observed: India as Viewed by British Artists, 1760–1860* (London: Victoria and Albert Museum, 1982), p. 84.

19 Kate Teltscher, *India Inscribed: European and British Writing on India, 1600–1800* (New Delhi: Oxford University Press, 1995), p. 129.

20 Quoted in Archer, *India and British Portraiture*, p. 239.

21 Quoted in Archer, *India and British Portraiture*, p. 206.

22 Quoted in P. J. Marshall, 'Warren Hastings as Scholar and Patron', in Anne Whiteman, J. S. Bromley and P. G. M. Dickson (eds), *Statesmen, Scholars and Merchants: Essays in Eighteenth-Century History Presented to Dame Lucy Sutherland* (Oxford: Clarendon Press, 1973), pp. 242–62, p. 256.

23 *Monthly Review*, 23 (August 1797), p. 408, quoted in Teltscher, *India Inscribed*, pp. 193–4.

24 William Jones, 'On the Gods of Greece, Italy and India', in P. J. Marshall (ed.), *The British Discovery of Hinduism in the Eighteenth Century* (Cambridge: Cambridge University Press, 1970), pp. 201–3.

CHAPTER 5

1 Quoted in Mildred Archer, *Indian Architecture and the British* (London: Country Life, 1968), p. 17.

2 Tillman W. Nechtman, 'Mr Hickey's Pictures: Britons and their Collectibles in Late Eighteenth-Century India', in Barry Crosbie and Mark Hampton (eds), *The Cultural Construction of the British World* (Manchester: Manchester University Press, 2015), pp. 180–97, p. 193.

3 Humphry Repton, *An Enquiry into the Changes of Taste in Landscape Gardening and Architecture* (London: J. Taylor, 1806), p. 41.

4 Royal Academy of Arts, London, Ozias Humphry papers (RAA), HU/3/13, Sir Robert Palk to Ozias Humphry, 7 December 1784; HU/3/21, Sir George Yonge to Sir John Dalling, 20 December 1784.

5 RAA, HU/3/30, Ozias Humphry to Mary Boydell, 16 May 1785.

6 Quoted in Georgina Green, *Sir Charles Raymond of Valentines and the East India Company* (London: Hainault Press, 2015), p. 89.

7 Quoted in Nechtman, 'Mr Hickey's Pictures', p. 193.

8 Quoted in P. J. Marshall, 'Taming the Exotic: The British and India in the Seventeenth and Eighteenth Centuries', in G. S. Rousseau and Roy Porter (eds), *Exoticism in the Enlightenment* (Manchester: Manchester University Press, 1990), pp. 46–65, p. 52.

9 Thomas Twining, *Travels in India a Hundred Years Ago* (London: Osgood, McIlvaine and Co., 1893), p. 348.

10 Quoted in Mildred Archer, 'British Patrons of Indian Artists', *Country Life* 118 (18 August 1955), pp. 340–1, p. 340.

11 Maria Graham, *Journal of a Residence in India* (Edinburgh: Archibald Constable, 1812), p. 146, quoted in Mildred Archer, *Natural History Drawings in the India Office Library* (London: HMSO, 1962), p. 56.

12 See Toby Falk and Mildred Archer, *Indian Miniatures in the India Office Library* (London: Sotheby Parke Bernet, 1981), pp. 17–23.

13 British Library, Add. Or. 1098–1235.

14 Ian Woodfield, *Music of the Raj: A Social and Economic History of Music in Late Eighteenth-Century Anglo-Indian Society* (Oxford: Oxford University Press, 2000), p. 196.

15 RAA, HU/3/36–7, Ozias Humphry to Mary Boydell, 7 August 1785.

16 RAA, HU/3/67–9, Ozias Humphry to Mary Boydell, 29 November 1786.

17 Mark Bence-Jones, 'A Nabob's Choice of Art: Clive of India as Builder and Collector', *Country Life* 150 (25 November 1971), pp. 1446–8, p. 1448.

18 Diary entry, 25 February 1818, in *The Diary of Joseph Farington*, edited by Kathryn Cave (New Haven and London: Yale University Press, 1984), vol. 15, p. 5162.

19 William Hickey, *Memoirs of William Hickey*, edited by Alfred Spencer, 4 vols (London: Hurst and Blackett, 1948), vol. 3, p. 342.

20 Hickey, *Memoirs*, vol. 4, p. 384.

21 Hickey, *Memoirs*, vol. 4, p. 387.

22 Quoted in Mildred Archer, *India and British Portraiture, 1770–1825* (London: Sotheby's, 1979), p. 229.

23 Quoted in Archer, *India and British Portraiture*, p. 230.

24 See Anna Winterbottom, *Hybrid Knowledge in the Early East India Company World* (Basingstoke: Palgrave Macmillan, 2016), p. 16.

25 Quoted in Natasha Eaton, *Mimesis across Empires: Artworks and Networks in India, 1765–1860* (Durham, NC: Duke University Press, 2013), p. 292, n. 12.

26 Quoted in Mildred Archer, *The India Office Collection of Paintings and Sculpture* (London: British Library, 1986), p. 84.

27 Quoted in Mildred Archer, 'The East India Company and British Art', *Apollo* 82 (1965), pp. 401–9, p. 406.

28 Quoted in Archer, 'The East India Company and British Art', p. 407.

29 Quoted in C. A. Bayly (ed.), *Raj: The British and India* (London: National Portrait Gallery, 1990), p. 101.

30 Quoted in William Foster, *The East India House: Its History and Associations* (London: John Lane, 1924), p. 133.

31 Sir John Fielding, *Description of London* (1776), p. 11, quoted in Green, *Sir Charles Raymond*, pp. 79–80.

32 Quoted in H. V. Bowen, 'The Most Illustrious and Most Flourishing Commercial Organisation that Ever Existed: The East India Company's Seaborne Empire, 1709–1833', in H. V. Bowen, John McAleer and Robert J. Blyth, *Monsoon Traders: The Maritime World of the East India Company* (London: Scala, 2011), pp. 91–125, pp. 96–7.

33 Joan Coutu, *Persuasion and Propaganda: Monuments and the Eighteenth-Century British Empire* (Montreal and Kingston: McGill-Queen's University Press, 2006), p. 287.

CHAPTER 6

1 Quoted in Jeremiah P. Losty, *Calcutta, City of Palaces: A Survey of the City in the Days of the East India Company, 1690–1858* (London: British Library, 1990), p. 76.

2 William Hickey, *Memoirs of William Hickey*, edited by Alfred Spencer, 4 vols (London: Hurst and Blackett, 1948), vol. 4, p. 236.

3 Thomas Pownall, *The Rights, Interest and Duty of Government, as Concerned in the Affairs of the East Indies* (London: J. Almon, 1773), p. 3.

4 British Library, Eg. MS 218, ff. 149–51, quoted in H. V. Bowen, *Revenue and Reform: The Indian Problem in British Politics, 1757–1773* (Cambridge: Cambridge University Press, 1991), p. 15.

5 Quoted in Losty, *Calcutta, City of Palaces*, p. 102.

6 Quoted in Pratapaditya Pal and Vidya Dehejia, *From Merchants to Emperors: British Artists and India, 1757–1930* (Ithaca and London: Cornell University Press, 1986), p. 146.

7 Claudius Buchanan, *Memoir of the Expediency of an Ecclesiastical Establishment for British India* (London: T. Cadell and W. Davies, 1805), p. xii, quoted in Rowan Strong, *Anglicanism and the British Empire, c. 1700–1850* (Oxford: Oxford University Press, 2007), p. 158.

FURTHER READING AND OTHER RESOURCES

Philip Lawson comments in the foreword to his general history of the East India Company that 'it would take several lifetimes to read all that exists today' on the subject (Philip Lawson, *The East India Company: A History* (London: Longman, 1993), p. viii). The literature on the Company – the principal commercial and political conduit connecting India and Britain for over two centuries – is vast, and it continues to grow. Indeed, in recent years, scholarly interest in the activities of this company, and its influence on the development of the British Empire, has expanded exponentially. In addition to Lawson's book, readers with an interest in the general history of the Company will find useful introductions in: John Keay, *The Honourable Company: A History of the English East India Company* (London: HarperCollins, 1993); Nick Robins, *The Corporation that Changed the World* (London: Pluto Press, 2006); Anthony Farrington, *Trading Places: The East India Company and Asia, 1600–1834* (London: British Library, 2002); H. V. Bowen, John McAleer and Robert J. Blyth, *Monsoon Traders: The Maritime World of the East India Company* (London: Scala, 2011).

More detailed studies of the complex relationship between the East India Company, British rule in India and the history of the British Empire more generally can be found in the work of P. J. Marshall and H. V. Bowen. See, for example, P. J. Marshall, 'British Expansion in India: A Historical Revision', *History* 60 (1975), pp. 28–43; P. J. Marshall, *East Indian Fortunes: The British in Bengal in the Eighteenth Century* (Oxford: Clarendon Press, 1976); P. J. Marshall, *Bengal: The British Bridgehead: Eastern India, 1740–1828* (Cambridge: Cambridge University Press, 2006); H. V. Bowen, *Revenue and Reform: The Indian Problem in British Politics, 1757–1773* (Cambridge: Cambridge University Press, 1991); H. V. Bowen, *The Business of Empire: The East India Company and Imperial Britain, 1756–1833* (Cambridge: Cambridge University Press, 2005).

On the history of the British engagement with India more generally, see Kate Teltscher, *India Inscribed: European and British Writing on India, 1600–1800* (New Delhi: Oxford University Press, 1995); P. J. Marshall and Glyndwr Williams, *The Great Map of Mankind: British Perceptions of the World in the Age of Enlightenment* (Cambridge, MA: Harvard University Press, 1982), especially pp. 67–184; Douglas M. Peers and Nandini Gooptu (eds), *India and the British Empire* (Oxford: Oxford University Press, 2012); C. A. Bayly, *Indian Society and the Making of the British Empire* (Cambridge: Cambridge University Press, 1988). On the wider imperial context, see P. J. Marshall, *The Making and Unmaking of Empires: Britain, India, and America, c. 1750–1783* (Oxford: Oxford University Press, 2005) and C. A. Bayly, *Imperial Meridian: The British Empire and the World, 1780–1830* (London: Longman, 1989).

The India Office Records at the British Library is the official repository of the East India Company's archives. In addition to fourteen kilometres of shelves containing official documents, letters and journals, the British Library also holds the world's premier collection of visual images recording the British encounter with the subcontinent. *Picturing India* draws on these unparalleled resources, highlighting the riches of the collection. In terms of other manuscripts sources, the letters of Ozias Humphry, in the collection of the Royal Academy of Arts, were useful in adding personal detail and offering the perspective of one artist who made the long and arduous journey to India in pursuit of fame and fortune.

A number of publications have explored facets of the British visual representation of India before. Sir William Foster offered one of the earliest accounts in a long article on 'British Artists in India, 1760–1820', which appeared in the *Walpole Society* over eighty years ago (vol. 19 (1930–1), pp. 1–88). *Picturing India* builds most obviously on the magisterial work of Mildred Archer, formerly of the India Office Library. Her most impressive books, such as *Company Drawings in the India Office Library* (London: HMSO, 1972), *India and British Portraiture, 1770–1825* (London: Sotheby's, 1979) and *The India Office Collection of Paintings and Sculpture* (London: British Library, 1986), are long out of print. However, their erudition has provided the basis for most of the subsequent scholarship on the subject. These books were complemented by a series of articles, all of which were useful in writing this book. See, for example, 'British Patrons of Indian Artists', *Country Life* 118 (18 August 1955), pp. 340–1, and 'The East India Company and British Art', *Apollo* 82 (1965), pp. 401–9.

A number of well-illustrated catalogues have been published over the years. See Mildred Archer and Ronald Lightbown, *India Observed: India as Viewed by British Artists, 1760–1860* (London: Victoria and Albert Museum, 1982); Pratapaditya Pal and Vidya Dehejia, *From Merchants to Emperors: British Artists and India, 1757–1930* (Ithaca and London: Cornell University Press, 1986); Anna Jackson and Amin Jaffer (eds), *Encounters: The Meeting of Asia and Europe, 1500–1800* (London: V&A Publications, 2004). One of the most important exhibitions in recent times to explore the complex interactions between the East India Company, Britain, and India was *The Raj: India and the British, 1600–1947*, held at the National Portrait Gallery in 1990. It confronted the complexities of this history, and the material culture and visual representations it produced. The exhibition tackled themes of representation through the selection, display and juxtaposition of a range of paintings, miniatures and other objects. The accompanying catalogue, *Raj: The British and India* (London: National Portrait Gallery, 1990), edited by C. A. Bayly, brings together a wealth of visual material that sheds light on Britain's centuries-long encounter and engagement with the subcontinent.

More recent studies include Hermione de Almeida and George H. Gilpin, *Indian Renaissance: British Romantic Art and the Prospect of India* (Farnham: Ashgate, 2006); Romita Ray, *Under the Banyan Tree: Relocating the Picturesque in British India* (New Haven and London: Yale University Press, 2013); Natasha Eaton, *Mimesis across Empires: Artworks and Networks in India, 1765–1860* (Durham, NC: Duke University Press, 2013). On Mughal art, and the influence of East India Company activity on Indian art more generally, see Jeremiah P. Losty and Malini Roy, *Mughal India: Art, Culture and Empire* (London: British Library, 2012).

PLACES

For a general introduction to the history, meaning and interpretation of landscape in Western art, see Malcolm Andrews, *Landscape and Western Art* (Oxford: Oxford University Press, 1999). For an excellent overview of the representation of landscape across almost the entire geographical range of the British Empire, see John E. Crowley, *Imperial Landscapes: Britain's Global Visual Culture, 1745–1820* (New Haven and London: Yale University Press, 2011). Chapter 6 of Crowley's book (pp. 169–203) deals specifically with India. For further discussion in relation to the representation of landscape by British artists in India, see Pauline Rohatgi and Pheroza Godrej (eds), *Under the Indian Sun: British Landscape Artists* (Bombay: Marg, 1995); Giles Tillotson, *The Artificial Empire: The Indian Landscapes of William Hodges* (London: Curzon, 2000); Romita Ray, *Under the Banyan Tree: Relocating the Picturesque in British India* (New Haven and London: Yale University Press, 2013). On Calcutta, see Jeremiah P. Losty, *Calcutta, City of Palaces: A Survey of the City in the Days of the East India Company, 1690–1858* (London: British Library, 1990). On the Taj Mahal, see Giles Tillotson, *Taj Mahal* (London: Profile Books, 2010). On Benares, see W. G. Archer, 'Benares through the Eyes of British Artists', *Apollo* 92 (1970), pp. 96–103. On architecture, see Mildred Archer, *Indian Architecture and the British* (London: Country Life, 1968), and Philip Davies, *Splendours of the Raj: British Architecture in India, 1660–1947* (London: Penguin, 1987).

PORTRAITS AND PEOPLE

There are a number of useful introductions to the subject of portraiture in general. See, for example, Shearer West, *Portraiture* (Oxford: Oxford University Press, 2004); Richard Brilliant, *Portraiture* (London: Reaktion Books, 1991); Joanna Woodall (ed.), *Portraiture: Facing the Subject* (Manchester: Manchester University Press, 1997). For the British context in particular, see Marcia Pointon, *Hanging the Head: Portraiture and Social Formation in Eighteenth-Century England* (New Haven and London: Yale University Press, 1993), and Kate Retford, *The Art of Domestic Life: Family Portraiture in Eighteenth-Century England* (New Haven and London: Yale University Press, 2006). The most comprehensive study of portraiture by European artists in the days of the East India Company remains Mildred Archer's *India and British Portraiture, 1770–1825* (London: Sotheby's, 1979). Beth Fowkes Tobin's book, *Picturing Imperial Power: Colonial Subjects in Eighteenth-Century British Painting* (London: Duke University Press, 1999), is also valuable. See especially chapter 4, 'Accommodating India: Domestic Arrangements in Anglo-Indian Family Portraiture', pp. 110–38. Other helpful texts include Mildred Archer and Ronald Lightbown, *India Observed: India as Viewed by British Artists, 1760–1860* (London: Victoria and Albert Museum, 1982), and Natasha Eaton, 'The Art of Colonial Despotism: Portraits, Politics and Power in South India, 1750–1795', *Cultural Critique* 70 (2008), pp. 63–93. On Indian miniatures, see Toby Falk and Mildred Archer, *Indian Miniatures in the India Office Library* (London: Sotheby Parke Bernet, 1981).

The *Oxford Dictionary of National Biography* (www.oxforddnb.com) provides an unrivalled source for details on the lives of individual British artists and sitters. There are also a number of specialist studies dedicated to individual artists discussed in *Picturing India*. See, for example, Geoff Quilley and John Bonehill (eds), *William Hodges, 1744–1797: The Art of Exploration* (London: National Maritime Museum, 2004); Thomas Sutton, *The Daniells: Artists and Travellers* (London: Bodley Head, 1954); Mildred Archer, *Early Views of India: The Picturesque Journeys of Thomas and William Daniell, 1786–1794* (London: Thames and Hudson, 1980); Jagmohan Mahajan, *Picturesque India: Sketches and Travels of Thomas and William Daniell* (New Delhi: Lustre Press, 1983); *An Illustrated Journey Round the World by Thomas, William & Samuel Daniell* (London: Folio Society, 2007), introduced and edited by Katherine Prior; Mildred Archer, 'Baltazard [*sic*] Solvyns and the Indian Picturesque', *Connoisseur* 170 (1969), pp. 12–18; Mildred Archer and Toby Falk, *The Passionate Quest: The Fraser Brothers in India* (London: Scorpion, 1989). As noted above, the letters of Ozias Humphry in the Royal Academy were also useful.

For an interesting study of a single individual, and his multiple influences on the history of the East India Company, see Georgina Green, *Sir Charles Raymond of Valentines and the East India Company* (London: Hainault Press, 2015). And, on the issue of using individual biographies to make wider points about the history of the British Empire in India, see Margot Finn, 'Anglo-Indian Lives in the Later Eighteenth and Early Nineteenth Century', *Journal for Eighteenth-Century Studies* 33 (2010), pp. 49–65.

The history of the nabobs is told in the work of a number of scholars. See, in particular, Percival Spear, *The Nabobs: A Study of the Social Life of the English in Eighteenth-Century India* (London: Oxford University Press, 1932); Tillman W. Nechtman, 'A Jewel in the Crown? Indian Wealth in Domestic Britain in the Late Eighteenth Century', *Eighteenth Century Studies* 41 (2007), pp. 71–86; Tillman W. Nechtman, *Nabobs: Empire and Identity in Eighteenth-Century Britain* (Cambridge: Cambridge University Press, 2010); Tillman W. Nechtman, 'Mr Hickey's Pictures: Britons and their Collectibles in Late Eighteenth-Century India', in Barry Crosbie and Mark Hampton (eds), *The Cultural Construction of the British World* (Manchester: Manchester University Press, 2015), pp. 180–97. Readers might also consult Suresh Chandra Ghosh's *The British in Bengal: A Study of the British Society and Life in the Late Eighteenth Century* (Leiden: Brill, 2007), and Michael Edwardes, *The Nabobs at Home* (London: Constable, 1991).

PATRONAGE

For further details on the history of East India House, see William Foster, *The East India House: Its History and Associations* (London: John Lane, 1924); William Foster, *John Company* (London: Bodley Head, 1926); H. V. Bowen, 'The Most Illustrious and Most Flourishing Commercial Organisation that Ever Existed: The East India Company's Seaborne Empire, 1709–1833', in H. V. Bowen, John McAleer and Robert J. Blyth, *Monsoon Traders: The Maritime World of the East India Company* (London: Scala, 2011), pp. 91–125, pp. 95–9. For the furnishings and internal decoration of East India House in the eighteenth century, see Mildred Archer, *The India Office Collection of Paintings and Sculpture* (London: British Library, 1986); John Hardy, *India Office Furniture* (London: British Library, 1982). For Government House in Calcutta, see Jeremiah P. Losty, *Calcutta, City of Palaces: A Survey of the City in the Days of the East India Company, 1690–1858* (London: British Library, 1990), pp. 71–80.

On collecting, patronage and the arts more generally, see Mildred Archer, 'British Patrons of Indian Artists', *Country Life* 118 (18 August 1955), pp. 340–1; P. J. Marshall, 'Warren Hastings as Scholar and Patron', in Anne Whiteman, J. S. Bromley and P. G. M. Dickson (eds), *Statesmen, Scholars and Merchants: Essays in Eighteenth-Century History presented to Dame Lucy Sutherland* (Oxford: Clarendon Press, 1973), pp. 242–62; Mark Bence-Jones, 'A Nabob's Choice of Art: Clive of India as Builder and Collector', *Country Life* 150 (25 November 1971), pp. 1446–8; Geoff Quilley, 'Signs of Commerce: The East India Company and the Patronage of Eighteenth-Century British Art', in H. V. Bowen, Margarette Lincoln and Nigel Rigby (eds), *The Worlds of the East India Company* (Woodbridge: Boydell, 2002), pp. 183–99; Joan Coutu, *Persuasion and Propaganda: Monuments and the Eighteenth-Century British Empire* (Montreal and Kingston: McGill-Queen's University Press, 2006), chapter 9, 'India: Empire Building as a Moral Imperative', pp. 270–321; Maya Jasanoff, *Edge of Empire: Conquest and Collecting in the East, 1750–1850* (London: Fourth Estate, 2005). On the impact of the Company on domestic contexts in Britain, and the way in which Asian luxury goods came to shape the British country house, see the 'East India Company at Home, 1757–1857' project run by Margot Finn, Helen Clifford, Kate Smith and Ellen Filor (http://blogs.ucl.ac.uk/eicah/home/).

For the paintings of George Lambert and Samuel Scott in the Directors' Court Room, see Brian Allen, 'The East India Company's Settlement Pictures: George Lambert and Samuel Scott', in Pauline Rohatgi and Pheroza Godrej (eds), *Under the Indian Sun: British Landscape Artists* (Bombay: Marg, 1995), pp. 1–16. For more on natural history drawings from India, see Mildred Archer, *Natural History Drawings in the India Office Library* (London: HMSO, 1962). For the definitive history of the East India Museum, see Ray Desmond, *The India Museum, 1801–1879* (London: HMSO, 1982). The article by Robert Skelton is also valuable: 'The Indian Collections: 1798 to 1978', *Burlington Magazine* 120 (1978), pp. 297–304. For more on the representation of the Company, from the eighteenth century up to the present day, see John McAleer, 'Displaying its Wares: Material Culture, the East India Company and British Encounters with India in the Long Eighteenth Century', in Gabriel Sánchez Espinosa, Daniel Roberts and Simon Davies (eds), *Global Connections: India and Europe in the Long Eighteenth Century* (Oxford: Voltaire Foundation, 2014), pp. 199–221.

INDEX

Italic page numbers refer to illustrations.